# Crucial Risk Taking

## Vision for the Book

"Crucial Risk Taking" is a profound exploration of the essential role risk plays in achieving both personal and professional success. In a world that often prioritizes safety and comfort, this book aims to challenge readers to reframe their perceptions of risk, viewing it not as a daunting obstacle but as a vital and rewarding component of their journey. It guides readers through the process of understanding the immense value that lies in stepping outside their comfort zones, taking calculated risks, and embracing uncertainty as a pathway to growth and transformation.

Through a rich tapestry of relatable stories, actionable strategies, and thought-provoking insights, "Crucial Risk Taking" seeks to resonate deeply on an emotional level. Readers will see themselves in the narratives shared, connecting their own fears and aspirations with the tangible steps outlined in the book. Each chapter is designed to help readers build confidence and clarity, transforming their approach to decision-making and empowering them to make bold, informed choices.

By the end of this journey, readers will have gained a new perspective on risk. They will understand that it is not a reckless gamble but a series of thoughtful actions that, when taken with intention and preparation, lead to extraordinary opportunities and achievements. "Crucial Risk Taking" will equip readers with the tools and mindset needed to navigate the uncertainties of life, turning potential fear into a powerful force for achieving their dreams and leading a more fulfilling, courageous life.

## Target Audience

"Crucial Risk Taking" is designed for individuals who are eager to break free from the constraints of their comfort zones and reach new heights of success and fulfillment. This book is particularly tailored for professionals, entrepreneurs, and aspiring leaders who are at a crossroads, facing the challenge of making bold decisions in a world that often prioritizes security and stability over innovation and progress.

These readers are driven by a deep-seated desire to make significant changes in their lives, achieve their goals, and leave a lasting impact on their communities and industries. They are visionaries and doers, yet they may find themselves grappling with common barriers such as fear of failure, indecision, or a lack of confidence. These obstacles can feel overwhelming, leading to hesitation and missed opportunities.

"Crucial Risk Taking" addresses these challenges head-on by providing practical advice, inspiring real-life stories, and a supportive, relatable tone that speaks directly to the reader's experiences and emotions. The book offers a roadmap for navigating the complexities of risk, turning fear into a source of strength and confidence. By engaging with the content, readers will find themselves equipped with the tools and mindset needed to take calculated risks that can transform their personal and professional lives.

In essence, this book is for anyone who is ready to embrace the unknown, challenge the status quo, and pursue their aspirations with renewed vigor and clarity. Whether they are looking to launch a new venture, pivot their career, or make a significant life change, "Crucial Risk Taking" will serve as their trusted guide and companion on the journey to achieving their fullest potential.

## Content

### Introduction

- **Outline**:
    - Connecting with the reader's journey and common fears about risk
    - The purpose and vision of the book
    - Overview of what readers can expect to gain
    - A brief anecdote or story to illustrate the power of taking risks

### Chapter 1: The Essence of Risk

- **Outline**:
    - Defining risk and its importance in life
    - Historical examples of great risks that led to success
    - The psychology of risk-taking
    - Personal reflections on understanding and embracing risk

### Chapter 2: The Fear Factor

- **Outline**:
    - Identifying common fears related to risk
    - Strategies for overcoming fear and building confidence
    - Real-life stories of individuals who conquered their fears
    - Exercises to help readers face and mitigate their own fears

### Chapter 3: Calculated Risks

- **Outline**:
    - Understanding the difference between reckless and calculated risks
    - Tools and frameworks for assessing risk
    - Case studies of successful calculated risks
    - Practical tips for making informed decisions

### Chapter 4: Overcoming Obstacles

- **Outline**:
    - Common challenges faced when taking risks
    - Strategies for resilience and perseverance
    - Stories of overcoming setbacks

- o Techniques for maintaining motivation and focus

## Chapter 5: The Mindset of a Risk Taker

- **Outline**:
    - o Developing a growth mindset
    - o The importance of adaptability and learning from failure
    - o Practices to cultivate a risk-taking mentality
    - o Inspirational quotes and affirmations

## Chapter 6: Building a Support System

- **Outline**:
    - o The role of mentors, peers, and networks in risk-taking
    - o How to find and cultivate a supportive community
    - o Examples of successful support systems
    - o Tips for giving and receiving support

## Chapter 7: Embracing Uncertainty

- **Outline**:
    - o The benefits of living with uncertainty
    - o Techniques for staying calm and focused in uncertain times
    - o Stories of individuals who thrived in uncertainty
    - o Exercises to practice embracing uncertainty

## Chapter 8: Measuring Success

- **Outline**:

- Redefining success beyond traditional metrics
- How to evaluate the outcomes of risks
- Examples of unexpected successes
- Encouraging readers to celebrate small wins

**Chapter 9: Sustaining Momentum**

- **Outline**:
    - Strategies for continuous improvement and risk-taking
    - Avoiding complacency and staying proactive
    - Long-term planning and goal setting
    - Inspirational stories of sustained success

**Chapter 10: Legacy and Impact**

- **Outline**:
    - The long-term impact of taking risks
    - How risk-taking shapes personal and professional legacy
    - Stories of influential risk-takers
    - Encouraging readers to think about their own legacy

**Conclusion**

- **Outline**:
    - Recap of the key takeaways from the book
    - Final thoughts on the importance of risk-taking
    - Motivational message to empower readers to take action

- A call to action for readers to start their own journey of risk-taking

# Introduction

## Connecting with the Reader's Journey and Common Fears about Risk

Imagine standing at the edge of a precipice, your heart pounding, palms sweating, and a mix of excitement and fear coursing through your veins. This is the moment of risk, a moment we all encounter in various forms throughout our lives. Whether it's changing careers, starting a new business, or even pursuing a personal passion, the fear of the unknown can be paralyzing. Yet, it is in these very moments that we find the greatest opportunities for growth, transformation, and success.

Taking risks is an intrinsic part of the human experience. From the first steps of a toddler to the monumental leaps in our personal and professional lives, risk is ever-present. But despite its omnipresence, many of us are held back by fear—fear of failure, fear of the unknown, and fear of stepping outside our comfort zones. This book is here to change that perspective.

Through "Crucial Risk Taking," we will embark on a journey to understand and conquer these fears. We will explore how embracing risk can lead to profound personal and professional growth. By sharing relatable stories and actionable strategies, this book aims to help you connect your fears and aspirations with tangible steps toward a more fulfilling and courageous life. Whether you're on the brink of a major life decision or simply looking to infuse more boldness into your everyday actions, this book will guide you in turning those moments of hesitation into catalysts for success.

## The Purpose and Vision of the Book

"Crucial Risk Taking" is a profound exploration of the essential role risk plays in achieving both personal and professional success. In a world that often prioritizes safety and comfort, this book aims to challenge readers to reframe their perceptions of risk, viewing it not as a daunting obstacle but as a vital and rewarding component of their journey.

The purpose of this book is to guide you through the process of understanding the immense value that lies in stepping outside your comfort zone. By taking calculated risks and embracing uncertainty, you open yourself up to a pathway of growth and transformation. This book is designed to help you recognize that risk is not something to be feared, but rather a necessary and empowering element of any significant achievement.

Through a combination of insightful strategies, relatable stories, and practical advice, "Crucial Risk Taking" will equip you with the tools needed to face challenges head-on. You will learn to see risks as opportunities for development and success, rather than threats to be avoided. The vision of this book is to foster a mindset where calculated risks become a natural and integral part of your decision-making process, leading to a more fulfilling and accomplished life.

## Overview of What Readers Can Expect to Gain

Throughout "Crucial Risk Taking," you can expect to gain actionable insights, practical strategies, and inspirational stories that will help you navigate the complex landscape of risk. This book is designed to delve deeply into the essence of risk, uncovering the fears that often hold us back and exploring the psychology behind our decisions. By understanding these fundamental aspects, you will be better prepared to face and embrace risks in your own life.

We will provide you with a variety of tools and frameworks for assessing risks, ensuring that you can make informed and calculated decisions. You'll discover historical and contemporary examples of successful risk-taking, offering you both inspiration and practical lessons. Additionally, this book will guide you in building a supportive network, emphasizing the importance of mentors, peers, and a community that encourages your risk-taking endeavors.

By the end of this journey, you will have a new perspective on risk. You will understand that it is not a reckless gamble but a series of thoughtful actions that, when taken with intention and preparation, lead to extraordinary opportunities and achievements. You will be equipped with the knowledge, confidence, and inspiration to take those crucial risks that will lead you to a more fulfilling and successful future. This book aims to transform your approach to risk, empowering you to harness it as a powerful tool for personal and professional growth.

## A Brief Anecdote or Story to Illustrate the Power of Taking Risks

To illustrate the power of taking risks, let me share a brief story. Several years ago, I found myself at a crossroads. I had a stable job that offered security but little satisfaction. Each day felt like I was merely going through the motions, and deep down, I knew there was more to life than the comfort of routine. The idea of venturing into entrepreneurship had always intrigued me, but the fear of failure loomed large, casting a shadow over my dreams.

After much contemplation and countless sleepless nights, I decided to take the plunge. I left my secure job and stepped into the unpredictable world of entrepreneurship. The path was fraught with challenges, from financial instability to the constant pressure of making my venture a success. There were moments of doubt, times when the fear seemed overwhelming, and I questioned my decision. But with each obstacle, I learned, adapted, and grew stronger.

The decision to embrace risk transformed my life in ways I could never have imagined. It brought professional success, yes, but more importantly, it brought a deep sense of personal fulfillment and a renewed passion for life. I discovered strengths I didn't know I had and experienced the joy of creating something from scratch.

This book is not just about my journey; it's about yours. It's about helping you realize that the most significant leaps often come with the greatest rewards. Together, we will explore how to make risk-taking a conscious, deliberate practice that can open doors to new possibilities and help you achieve your dreams.

So, let's embark on this journey together. Let's redefine risk, embrace it, and make it an integral part of our lives. By the end of this book, you'll be ready to take those crucial risks that will lead you to a more fulfilling and successful future.

# Chapter 1

# The Essence of Risk

## Defining Risk and Its Importance in Life

Risk is often perceived as something to be avoided, a perilous path that can lead to failure and disappointment. The very mention of risk can conjure images of loss, uncertainty, and potential danger. However, this perception overlooks a fundamental truth: risk is an integral part of growth and achievement. It is the willingness to step into the unknown, to challenge the status quo, and to pursue opportunities that are not guaranteed.

Without risk, there is no innovation, no progress, and no real achievement. Consider the milestones in human history that have shaped our world—each significant advancement has been born from the willingness to take a leap of faith. Risk is the bridge between where we are and where we aspire to be. It is the catalyst for change, the spark that ignites progress, and the foundation upon which success is built.

In our personal lives, risk manifests in various forms. It might be the decision to switch careers, move to a new city, start a business, or even express a long-held dream. These decisions are fraught with uncertainty and potential setbacks, but they are also the moments that define us, pushing us to discover new possibilities, push our boundaries, and achieve greatness.

Taking risks involves embracing vulnerability and stepping outside our comfort zones. It means acknowledging the possibility of failure but choosing to act despite it. This willingness to face the unknown is what drives personal and professional growth. When we take risks, we open ourselves up to learning, adaptation, and ultimately, transformation.

In essence, risk is not just a path fraught with potential pitfalls; it is also a path laden with opportunities. By redefining our relationship with risk, we can move from a mindset of fear to one of empowerment. We can start to see risk as a necessary and rewarding component of our journey toward achieving our fullest potential.

## Historical Examples of Great Risks that Led to Success

History is replete with examples of individuals who took monumental risks that led to groundbreaking success. These stories not only inspire but also underscore the vital role that risk plays in driving progress and innovation.

Consider the story of Thomas Edison, a prolific inventor whose relentless experimentation and willingness to embrace risk resulted in the creation of the electric light bulb. Edison faced numerous failures and setbacks, enduring over a thousand unsuccessful attempts before achieving success. Each failure was a step closer to his goal, and his persistence paid off with an invention that revolutionized the world. Edison's story exemplifies how embracing risk and learning from failure can lead to transformative achievements.

Similarly, the bold decision of explorers like Christopher Columbus serves as another powerful example. In 1492, Columbus ventured into uncharted waters, risking his life and the lives of his crew in the hope of discovering new lands. Despite the immense uncertainty and the potential for disaster, Columbus's courage and risk-taking spirit led to the discovery of the Americas. This monumental journey opened up new frontiers, reshaping human history and paving the way for further exploration and expansion.

Another notable example is the story of the Wright brothers, Orville and Wilbur Wright, who risked their reputations and financial stability to pursue the dream of powered flight. In an era when the idea of human flight was considered fantastical and impractical, the Wright brothers' dedication and willingness to face repeated failures and public skepticism eventually culminated in the first successful flight in 1903. Their achievement not only marked the birth of aviation but also demonstrated the profound impact of taking calculated risks to challenge the boundaries of possibility.

These historical examples illustrate that great risks often lead to great rewards. The individuals who dared to venture into the unknown and challenge conventional wisdom achieved feats that changed the course of history. Their stories remind us that risk-taking is an essential component of innovation and progress. By learning from their experiences, we can find the courage to embrace our own risks and pursue our dreams with determination and resilience.

## The Psychology of Risk-Taking

Understanding the psychology of risk-taking is crucial for anyone looking to embrace risk in their lives. Our brains are wired to seek safety and avoid danger, a survival mechanism that has served humanity well throughout evolution. This instinctual drive to protect ourselves from harm has been essential for our survival as a species. However, in the modern world, this same instinct can often hold us back from pursuing opportunities that involve uncertainty and potential reward.

One of the most significant psychological barriers to taking risks is the fear of failure. Failure is often perceived as a negative outcome, something to be avoided at all costs. This fear can paralyze us, preventing us from taking action and exploring new possibilities. However, it's important to recognize that failure is an integral part of the learning process. Each failure provides valuable insights and lessons that can guide us toward eventual success.

Another psychological barrier is the discomfort of stepping into the unknown. Humans are creatures of habit, and we find comfort in familiarity and routine. The unknown represents uncertainty and unpredictability, which can trigger anxiety and stress. Overcoming this discomfort requires a shift in mindset, viewing the unknown not as a threat but as an opportunity for growth and discovery.

The anxiety of potential loss is another factor that can deter us from taking risks. This loss aversion, the tendency to prefer avoiding losses over acquiring equivalent gains, is a powerful psychological phenomenon. It can lead us to overestimate the likelihood of negative outcomes and underestimate the potential benefits of taking a risk. By understanding this cognitive bias, we can work to counteract its effects and make more balanced decisions.

To manage these psychological barriers, we can develop several strategies. First, it's essential to reframe our perspective on failure, seeing it as a stepping stone rather than an endpoint. Building resilience involves embracing failure as part of the journey and learning to recover and adapt. Visualization techniques can also help, where we imagine the best and worst-case scenarios, helping to demystify the unknown and reduce anxiety.

Informed decision-making is another critical aspect of managing risk. By gathering relevant information, weighing the pros and cons, and considering potential outcomes, we can make more rational and less fear-driven decisions. Additionally, seeking support from mentors, peers, and a supportive community can provide valuable perspectives and encouragement.

By understanding the psychological factors that influence our approach to risk, we can develop strategies to manage fear, build resilience, and make informed decisions. Embracing risk becomes a more deliberate and calculated process, empowering us to pursue opportunities that lead to personal and professional growth.

## Personal Reflections on Understanding and Embracing Risk

Embracing risk is a deeply personal journey, one that requires introspection and self-awareness. Reflecting on our own experiences with risk can provide valuable insights into how we perceive and approach uncertainty. Each of us has a unique relationship with risk, shaped by our past experiences, upbringing, and individual mindset.

For me, the decision to leave a stable job and pursue entrepreneurship was a pivotal moment in my life. It was a choice fraught with uncertainty and potential pitfalls. I had to confront my fears head-on, weigh the potential outcomes, and ultimately take a leap of faith. This decision was not made lightly; it involved careful consideration and a willingness to step into the unknown.

Through this journey, I learned that risk is not about recklessness but about making calculated decisions that align with our values and aspirations. It required me to assess my goals, understand my motivations, and evaluate the potential rewards and challenges. By doing so, I was able to approach risk in a more informed and intentional manner.

Embracing risk has allowed me to grow, learn, and achieve things I once thought impossible. It has opened doors to new opportunities, fostered personal and professional development, and instilled a sense of resilience and adaptability. The experience taught me that taking risks is an essential part of living a fulfilling and meaningful life.

In this chapter, we will delve deeper into these aspects of risk. We will explore how defining and understanding risk can empower us to make bold decisions. By learning from historical examples and applying psychological insights, we can better navigate the complexities of risk in our own lives. Through personal reflections and practical advice, you will gain a comprehensive understanding of the essence of risk and how it can be harnessed to achieve your goals and dreams.

This journey is about more than just taking risks; it's about transforming our approach to decision-making and embracing the possibilities that come with stepping outside our comfort zones. Together, we will uncover the profound impact that calculated risk-taking can have on our lives and how it can lead to extraordinary growth and success.

# Chapter 2

# The Fear Factor

## Identifying Common Fears Related to Risk

Fear is a natural response to the unknown, and it often manifests when we are faced with taking risks. Some of the most common fears include:

- **Fear of Failure**
- Fear of failure is one of the most pervasive and paralyzing fears when it comes to taking risks. This anxiety stems from the possibility of not achieving our goals and the associated consequences, which can range from loss of reputation and financial instability to personal disappointment and diminished self-esteem.
- At its core, the fear of failure is deeply rooted in our desire for acceptance and success. Society often places a high value on achievements and accolades, and as a result, the prospect of failing can feel like a threat to our identity and worth. The fear of being judged or ridiculed by others can be overwhelming, leading many to avoid taking risks altogether.
- Financial instability is another significant concern tied to the fear of failure. Whether it's starting a new business, investing in a new venture, or making a career change, the financial implications of failure can be daunting. The thought of losing hard-earned money or facing financial hardship can deter even

the most ambitious individuals from pursuing their dreams.
- Personal disappointment is also a critical aspect of the fear of failure. The internalized pressure to succeed and meet our own expectations can create a fear of letting ourselves down. This self-imposed pressure can lead to a vicious cycle of procrastination and avoidance, preventing us from taking the necessary steps toward our goals.
- Despite its powerful hold, the fear of failure can be managed and overcome. Recognizing that failure is a natural and essential part of growth is the first step. Each failure provides valuable lessons and insights that can guide us toward future success. By reframing our perception of failure as a learning opportunity rather than a definitive end, we can reduce its paralyzing grip.
- It's also crucial to understand that failure does not define us. Our worth and identity are not contingent on our successes or failures. By separating our self-worth from our achievements, we can approach risks with a healthier mindset.
- Another effective strategy for managing the fear of failure is to set realistic and incremental goals. Breaking down larger objectives into smaller, manageable tasks can help build confidence and momentum. Achieving these smaller milestones provides a sense of accomplishment and reduces the overall anxiety associated with the larger goal.
- Seeking support from mentors, peers, and loved ones can also make a significant difference. Surrounding ourselves with a supportive network can provide encouragement, constructive feedback, and reassurance. Sharing our fears and challenges

with others can help normalize the experience of failure and reduce feelings of isolation.
- In conclusion, the fear of failure is a common and understandable barrier to taking risks. However, by recognizing its impact, reframing our perception of failure, setting realistic goals, and seeking support, we can manage this fear and move forward with greater confidence and resilience. Taking risks becomes not only possible but a vital part of achieving our goals and realizing our potential.

## Fear of the Unknown

Fear of the unknown is a powerful and often paralyzing emotion that arises from stepping into situations with uncertain outcomes, where we lack control and predictability. This fear is deeply rooted in our natural aversion to uncertainty and the discomfort it brings. When faced with the unknown, our minds can conjure up worst-case scenarios, amplifying our anxiety and making us hesitant to take action.

The discomfort of the unknown stems from the human brain's need for structure and predictability. We are wired to seek out patterns and make sense of our environment, which provides a sense of security and control. When we encounter situations where outcomes are uncertain, our brains struggle to process the ambiguity, leading to feelings of anxiety and stress.

This fear can manifest in various aspects of our lives, from career changes and new business ventures to personal relationships and moving to a new city. The common thread is the uncertainty about the future and the inability to foresee the consequences of our actions. This lack of control can be unsettling, causing us to shy away from opportunities that involve significant change or unpredictability.

However, fear of the unknown, like other fears, can be managed and even leveraged for personal growth. Here are several strategies to help mitigate this fear:

1. **Embrace Curiosity**: Shift your perspective from fearing the unknown to being curious about it. Curiosity can transform anxiety into a sense of adventure, allowing you to approach new situations with an open mind and a willingness to learn.
2. **Gather Information**: One way to reduce fear is to gather as much information as possible about the situation. Research, ask questions, and seek advice from others who have faced similar circumstances. Knowledge can demystify the unknown and provide a clearer picture of what to expect.
3. **Focus on What You Can Control**: While you may not have control over every aspect of an uncertain situation, identify the elements you can influence. By focusing on these areas, you can create a sense of stability and reduce anxiety.
4. **Visualize Positive Outcomes**: Instead of fixating on worst-case scenarios, practice visualizing positive outcomes. This can help shift your mindset from fear to optimism, making it easier to take action despite uncertainty.
5. **Take Small Steps**: Break down the larger unknown into smaller, manageable steps. Taking gradual, incremental actions can help build confidence and make the overall situation feel less overwhelming.

6. **Accept Uncertainty as Part of Life**: Recognize that uncertainty is an inherent part of life. Accepting this reality can help you develop a more resilient mindset, enabling you to navigate unknown situations with greater ease.
7. **Build a Support Network**: Surround yourself with supportive individuals who can provide guidance, encouragement, and reassurance. Sharing your fears and concerns with others can help normalize your feelings and reduce the sense of isolation.

By applying these strategies, you can begin to manage the fear of the unknown and turn it into an opportunity for growth and exploration. Embracing uncertainty allows you to discover new possibilities, push your boundaries, and achieve your goals. Remember, every significant achievement involves a degree of the unknown, and it is through facing these uncertainties that we grow and evolve.

## Fear of Rejection

Fear of rejection is a profound and often debilitating fear that many people experience. It is the apprehension that our ideas, proposals, or efforts will be dismissed or criticized by others, leading to a sense of inadequacy. This fear can significantly impact our willingness to take risks, as the potential for rejection can feel deeply personal and affect our self-esteem.

At its core, the fear of rejection is tied to our need for acceptance and validation. Humans are inherently social beings, and our sense of belonging is crucial to our emotional well-being. When we put ourselves out there—whether through sharing an idea, submitting a proposal, or making a bold move—we open ourselves up to the possibility of judgment and disapproval. The thought of being rejected can be so intimidating that it prevents us from taking action, thereby limiting our opportunities for growth and success.

The fear of rejection can manifest in various contexts, including the workplace, social situations, and personal relationships. In the professional realm, it might prevent us from pitching innovative ideas, applying for promotions, or seeking new job opportunities. In social settings, it can inhibit us from forming new connections or expressing our true selves. In personal relationships, the fear of rejection can lead to difficulties in communicating openly or pursuing meaningful relationships.

However, it is important to recognize that rejection is a natural and inevitable part of life. Everyone experiences rejection at some point, and it does not define our worth or capabilities. By reframing our perception of rejection and developing strategies to cope with it, we can mitigate its impact and continue to take risks that align with our goals and aspirations.

Here are some strategies to help manage the fear of rejection:

1. **Reframe Rejection**: View rejection as feedback rather than a personal indictment. Understand that rejection is often a reflection of circumstances, preferences, or external factors rather than your intrinsic value.
2. **Normalize Rejection**: Recognize that rejection is a common experience shared by everyone. Even the most successful individuals have faced rejection

multiple times. Normalizing this experience can reduce its emotional impact.
3. **Build Resilience**: Strengthen your resilience by focusing on your strengths and accomplishments. Remind yourself of past successes and how you overcame previous rejections. This can boost your confidence and help you bounce back more quickly.
4. **Seek Constructive Criticism**: Instead of avoiding feedback, actively seek constructive criticism. This approach can help you improve and grow, transforming rejection into an opportunity for development.
5. **Practice Self-Compassion**: Be kind to yourself when faced with rejection. Acknowledge your efforts and remind yourself that it is okay to experience setbacks. Self-compassion can help alleviate feelings of inadequacy and maintain a positive mindset.
6. **Take Small Risks**: Gradually expose yourself to situations where rejection is possible. Start with small, manageable risks and progressively take on larger challenges. This practice can help desensitize you to rejection and build confidence.
7. **Focus on the Process**: Shift your focus from the outcome to the process. Emphasize the value of taking action and putting yourself out there, regardless of the result. Celebrating your courage to take risks can diminish the fear of rejection.

By implementing these strategies, you can manage the fear of rejection and continue to pursue your goals with confidence and determination. Remember that rejection is not an end but a step in the journey toward achieving your dreams. Embracing the possibility of rejection allows you to take bold actions, learn from your experiences, and ultimately grow stronger and more resilient.

## Fear of Change

Fear of change is a common and deeply rooted apprehension that many people experience. It stems from the resistance to altering the status quo, which can disrupt our routines and force us to adapt to new circumstances. This fear can be particularly challenging because it involves stepping out of our comfort zones and facing the uncertainty that comes with new experiences.

At the heart of the fear of change is the human preference for stability and predictability. Our daily routines provide a sense of security and control, allowing us to navigate life with a degree of confidence. When faced with the prospect of change, this sense of stability is threatened, leading to feelings of anxiety and discomfort. The familiar, even if unsatisfactory, often feels safer than the unknown.

This fear can manifest in various aspects of life, including career transitions, personal relationships, and lifestyle changes. For instance, changing jobs or relocating to a new city involves leaving behind familiar environments and colleagues. Ending a long-term relationship or starting a new one requires adjusting to different dynamics and expectations. Even positive changes, such as promotions or new opportunities, can trigger fear because they necessitate adaptation and growth.

Understanding and addressing the fear of change is crucial for personal and professional development. Here are some strategies to help manage and overcome this fear:

1. **Acknowledge Your Feelings**: The first step in overcoming the fear of change is to acknowledge and accept your feelings. Understand that it is natural to feel apprehensive about stepping into the unknown. Validating your emotions can help you process them more effectively.
2. **Focus on the Benefits**: Shift your focus from the potential negatives to the positive outcomes that change can bring. Consider the opportunities for growth, learning, and improvement that come with new experiences. Visualizing the benefits can help reduce anxiety and increase motivation.
3. **Take Incremental Steps**: Gradual exposure to change can make the process less overwhelming. Break down the larger change into smaller, manageable steps. By taking incremental actions, you can build confidence and adaptability over time.
4. **Seek Support**: Surround yourself with supportive individuals who can provide encouragement and guidance. Sharing your concerns with trusted friends, family members, or mentors can help alleviate feelings of isolation and provide valuable perspectives.
5. **Develop a Flexible Mindset**: Cultivate a mindset that embraces flexibility and adaptability. Understand that change is an inherent part of life and that adapting to new circumstances can lead to personal growth and resilience.
6. **Learn from Past Experiences**: Reflect on previous instances where you successfully navigated change. Identify the strategies that helped you cope and apply those lessons to the current situation.

Recognizing your ability to handle change in the past can boost your confidence.
7. **Create a Plan**: Having a plan can provide a sense of control and reduce uncertainty. Outline the steps you need to take to navigate the change and set achievable goals. A clear plan can help you stay focused and organized.
8. **Practice Self-Compassion**: Be kind to yourself during times of change. Acknowledge that it is okay to feel uneasy and that adjusting to new circumstances takes time. Self-compassion can help you maintain a positive mindset and reduce self-criticism.

By implementing these strategies, you can manage the fear of change and approach new situations with greater confidence and resilience. Embracing change allows you to explore new possibilities, grow beyond your current limitations, and achieve your full potential. Remember, change is not something to be feared but an opportunity to evolve and thrive.

## Fear of Success

Surprisingly, the fear of achieving success can be just as paralyzing as the fear of failure. While success is often seen as the ultimate goal, it can bring with it a host of new challenges that can trigger anxiety and self-doubt. This fear of success may seem counterintuitive, but it is a real and significant barrier for many individuals.

One of the primary reasons people fear success is the increased responsibilities that come with it. Achieving success often means taking on more significant roles, managing larger teams, or handling more complex projects. This added responsibility can be daunting, as it requires a higher level of commitment, effort, and accountability. The pressure to maintain and build on one's success can lead to stress and overwhelm.

Higher expectations are another factor contributing to the fear of success. Once you achieve a certain level of success, there is often an expectation to continue performing at that high level. This can create a fear of not being able to sustain success, leading to anxiety about potential future failures. The thought of disappointing others or not living up to their expectations can be a significant source of stress.

The potential envy and resentment from others can also fuel the fear of success. Success can sometimes attract negative attention from peers, colleagues, or even friends and family. The fear of being judged, criticized, or isolated because of one's achievements can make the prospect of success less appealing. This social aspect of success can create a sense of isolation, as it may be challenging to find people who understand and support your journey.

Here are some strategies to help manage and overcome the fear of success:

1. **Acknowledge Your Fear**: Recognize and accept that fear of success is a legitimate concern. Understanding that it is a common experience can help you feel less isolated and more empowered to address it.
2. **Identify Specific Fears**: Break down your fear of success into specific concerns. Are you worried about increased responsibilities, higher expectations, or potential envy from others?

Identifying the root causes can help you address each aspect more effectively.
3. **Set Realistic Goals**: Establish clear, achievable goals that allow you to build on your success gradually. This approach can help you manage expectations and avoid feeling overwhelmed by the pressure to perform at a high level continuously.
4. **Seek Support**: Surround yourself with a supportive network of people who understand and encourage your aspirations. Mentors, coaches, and supportive peers can provide valuable guidance and reassurance as you navigate the challenges of success.
5. **Develop a Growth Mindset**: Embrace a mindset that views success as a continuous journey rather than a final destination. Understand that success involves ongoing learning, adaptation, and personal growth. This perspective can help reduce the pressure to achieve perfection and encourage a more balanced approach.
6. **Practice Self-Compassion**: Be kind to yourself as you navigate the complexities of success. Acknowledge your achievements and recognize that it is normal to experience doubts and fears. Self-compassion can help you maintain a positive mindset and build resilience.
7. **Manage Expectations**: Communicate openly with others about your boundaries and limitations. Managing expectations can help reduce the pressure to constantly perform at a high level and allow you to set realistic, achievable goals.
8. **Celebrate Your Successes**: Take time to acknowledge and celebrate your achievements, no

matter how small. Recognizing your progress can help reinforce your confidence and motivation.

By implementing these strategies, you can manage the fear of success and embrace the opportunities that come with it. Understanding that success is a multifaceted journey, complete with its challenges and rewards, can help you navigate it with confidence and resilience. Remember, achieving success is not just about reaching a goal but about growing, learning, and evolving along the way.

## Strategies for Overcoming Fear and Building Confidence

Overcoming fear is a process that requires intentional effort and practice. Here are some strategies to help you manage and mitigate fear:

- **Acknowledge Your Fears**
- The first step in overcoming fear is to recognize and acknowledge it. Fear is a natural and universal human emotion, and experiencing it does not signify weakness. Instead, it is an instinctual response that has evolved to help us navigate potential dangers and uncertainties in our environment. By acknowledging our fears, we can begin to understand and address them more effectively.
- Recognizing fear involves paying attention to the physical and emotional signals that accompany it. These may include a racing heart, sweaty palms, anxiety, or a sense of unease. When we become aware of these signs, we can identify the specific

fears that are holding us back, whether they relate to failure, rejection, change, or success.
- Acknowledging fear requires a level of self-honesty and vulnerability. It means admitting to ourselves that we are afraid and allowing ourselves to feel those emotions without judgment. This self-awareness is crucial because it lays the foundation for addressing and managing our fears. By bringing our fears into the open, we strip them of their power to control our actions subconsciously.
- Understanding that fear is a normal response is also essential. It is a common experience shared by everyone, regardless of their level of success or confidence. Even the most accomplished individuals experience fear, and it is often their ability to acknowledge and confront it that sets them apart. Recognizing that fear is a part of the human experience can help normalize it and reduce feelings of isolation.
- To acknowledge your fears, start by reflecting on situations that trigger anxiety or discomfort. Write down these fears in a journal, describing how they make you feel and how they impact your actions. This exercise can help you gain clarity and perspective on your fears, making them more tangible and less intimidating.
- Once you have identified your fears, talk about them with someone you trust. Sharing your fears with a friend, family member, or mentor can provide support and reassurance. It can also help you gain new insights and strategies for managing your fears from those who may have faced similar challenges.
- In summary, acknowledging your fears is the first critical step in overcoming them. By recognizing

and accepting your fears as a normal part of life, you can begin to address them with greater confidence and clarity. This process of acknowledgment sets the stage for the subsequent steps in managing and ultimately overcoming fear, allowing you to pursue your goals and dreams with resilience and determination.

- **Educate Yourself**
- Knowledge is a powerful antidote to fear. When we face uncertainty, our minds can fill in the gaps with worst-case scenarios and exaggerated risks. By gathering information and understanding the risks involved, we can demystify the unknown and significantly reduce anxiety.
- The process of educating yourself begins with thorough research. If you are contemplating a career change, starting a new business, or any other major life decision, start by seeking out as much information as possible. Read books, articles, and reports related to your area of interest. Attend workshops, seminars, and webinars that provide insights and expert opinions. The more you learn, the more you can replace fear with facts and clarity.
- In addition to written resources, talking to people who have already navigated similar paths can be incredibly beneficial. Reach out to mentors, colleagues, or professionals who have experience in the field you are exploring. Ask them about their experiences, the challenges they faced, and how they overcame them. Hearing firsthand accounts can provide a realistic perspective and practical advice that you might not find in written materials.
- Understanding the specifics of the risks involved is another crucial aspect of educating yourself. Break

down the potential risks into manageable components. For example, if you are considering starting a business, identify the financial, operational, and market risks. Analyze these risks individually to understand their implications and how you can mitigate them. This detailed approach can help you feel more in control and less overwhelmed by the overall uncertainty.
- Another effective strategy is to create a plan or roadmap. Outline the steps you need to take to move forward and achieve your goals. By having a clear plan, you can anticipate potential obstacles and prepare solutions in advance. This proactive approach can reduce the fear of unforeseen challenges and give you a sense of direction.
- Additionally, stay updated on the latest trends and developments in your area of interest. The world is constantly changing, and staying informed can help you adapt and make informed decisions. Subscribe to industry newsletters, join relevant online forums, and follow thought leaders on social media. Continuous learning will keep you ahead of the curve and reinforce your confidence.
- Lastly, practice critical thinking and question your assumptions. Often, fear is based on misconceptions or outdated beliefs. Challenge your thoughts by asking yourself if they are based on facts or unfounded fears. This reflective practice can help you identify irrational fears and replace them with a more balanced and informed perspective.
- In conclusion, educating yourself is a crucial step in overcoming fear. By gathering information, seeking advice, and understanding the risks involved, you

can demystify the unknown and reduce anxiety. Knowledge empowers you to make informed decisions, navigate uncertainties with confidence, and take bold steps toward achieving your goals.

- **Set Realistic Goals**
- Setting realistic goals is a crucial strategy for managing fear and building confidence. When faced with a significant challenge or ambition, the sheer scale of the task can be overwhelming. Breaking down larger goals into smaller, manageable steps can make the process less intimidating and more achievable. This approach not only helps to clarify your path forward but also allows you to celebrate incremental progress, building momentum and confidence along the way.
- Start by clearly defining your larger goal. This might be a long-term vision such as starting a business, changing careers, or achieving a personal milestone. Once you have a clear picture of what you want to achieve, break this goal down into smaller, actionable steps. Each step should be specific, measurable, and attainable within a reasonable timeframe.
- For example, if your goal is to start a new business, break it down into key phases such as market research, business planning, securing funding, and launching the product or service. Within each phase, identify specific tasks that need to be completed. For market research, tasks might include identifying target demographics, analyzing competitors, and surveying potential customers. For business planning, tasks might include writing a business plan, developing a marketing strategy, and setting financial projections.

- By breaking down your goal into these smaller tasks, you can focus on one step at a time, making the overall process less daunting. This step-by-step approach allows you to tackle each task with greater clarity and purpose, reducing the sense of overwhelm that can accompany large goals.
- Achieving these smaller milestones provides an opportunity to celebrate progress and build momentum. Each completed task is a tangible accomplishment that brings you one step closer to your larger goal. Celebrating these successes, no matter how small, can boost your confidence and motivation. It reinforces the idea that you are making progress and that your goal is within reach.
- Setting realistic goals also involves being flexible and adaptable. Recognize that the path to achieving your larger goal may not be linear. There may be setbacks, unexpected challenges, and changes in direction. By setting smaller, manageable goals, you can more easily adjust your plans and stay on track, even when obstacles arise.
- It's important to set goals that are challenging yet attainable. Goals that are too easy may not provide the motivation needed to push forward, while goals that are too difficult can lead to frustration and discouragement. Finding the right balance ensures that you stay motivated and engaged throughout the process.
- In addition to setting smaller goals, establish a timeline for achieving them. A timeline provides structure and a sense of urgency, helping you stay focused and committed. Regularly review your progress and adjust your timeline as needed to stay on track.

- In conclusion, setting realistic goals by breaking down larger objectives into smaller, manageable steps is a powerful strategy for overcoming fear and building confidence. Each small success reinforces your belief in your ability to achieve your larger goal, creating a positive cycle of momentum and motivation. By approaching your goals with clarity, flexibility, and persistence, you can turn your ambitions into reality and navigate the journey with greater ease and confidence.
- **Visualize Success**
- Positive visualization is a powerful technique that can help shift your focus from potential failure to potential achievement. By using visualization, you create a mental image of success, which can inspire confidence, reduce anxiety, and increase motivation. This practice harnesses the power of your mind to transform your outlook and prepare you for success.
- To start with visualization, find a quiet and comfortable place where you can relax without interruptions. Close your eyes and take a few deep breaths to center yourself. Once you are calm and focused, begin to imagine your goal in vivid detail. Picture yourself achieving success, and immerse yourself in the experience as if it is happening right now.
- Imagine the specific steps you will take to reach your goal. For instance, if you are preparing for an important presentation, visualize yourself confidently delivering your speech, engaging your audience, and responding to questions with ease. See yourself standing tall, speaking clearly, and exuding confidence. Visualize the positive reactions

of your audience, the sense of accomplishment you feel, and the praise you receive afterward.
- As you visualize, engage all your senses to make the experience as realistic as possible. Hear the sounds around you, feel the physical sensations, and see the vibrant colors and details of the environment. The more detailed and vivid your visualization, the more powerful it will be in shaping your mindset and emotions.
- Positive visualization can also be used to rehearse challenging scenarios and build resilience. If you are facing a difficult decision or anticipating obstacles, visualize yourself navigating these challenges successfully. Imagine how you will handle setbacks, maintain your composure, and find solutions. This mental rehearsal can prepare you for real-life situations and increase your confidence in handling adversity.
- Incorporating positive affirmations into your visualization practice can further enhance its effectiveness. Affirmations are positive statements that reinforce your belief in your abilities and the likelihood of success. As you visualize, repeat affirmations such as "I am capable of achieving my goals," "I handle challenges with grace and confidence," or "I am prepared for success." These affirmations can help reprogram your subconscious mind and reinforce a positive outlook.
- Consistent practice is key to making visualization a powerful tool for success. Set aside time each day to visualize your goals and reinforce positive outcomes. Over time, this practice can help you develop a success-oriented mindset, making it easier to take action and overcome fears.

- Research has shown that visualization can have tangible benefits for performance and achievement. Athletes, performers, and successful individuals across various fields use visualization to enhance their skills and achieve their goals. By visualizing success, you are training your brain to recognize and seize opportunities, boosting your confidence and increasing your chances of success.
- In conclusion, positive visualization is a valuable technique for shifting your focus from potential failure to potential achievement. By creating a mental image of success and rehearsing it in your mind, you can reduce anxiety, build confidence, and enhance your motivation. Incorporate visualization into your daily routine, and use it to prepare for challenges, reinforce positive outcomes, and inspire yourself to take bold actions toward achieving your goals.

## Seek Support

Seeking support is a vital strategy for overcoming fear and building confidence. Surrounding yourself with supportive people who encourage and believe in you can provide valuable guidance, reassurance, and motivation. These individuals can play a crucial role in helping you navigate challenges, maintain perspective, and stay committed to your goals.

1. **Mentors**: Mentors are experienced individuals who have navigated similar paths and can offer valuable insights and advice. They can help you anticipate potential obstacles, provide solutions based on their experiences, and offer encouragement when

you face setbacks. Mentors can also help you see the bigger picture, keeping you focused on your long-term goals and reminding you of your progress along the way. Finding a mentor who understands your aspirations and challenges can be a game-changer in your journey.

2. **Peers**: Your peers, especially those who share similar goals or are on a similar journey, can be a great source of support. They understand the challenges you face and can offer empathy, encouragement, and practical advice. Engaging with peers can create a sense of camaraderie and accountability, as you can motivate each other to stay on track and celebrate each other's successes. Peer support groups, professional networks, and mastermind groups are excellent ways to connect with like-minded individuals.

3. **Loved Ones**: Family and friends who care about your well-being can provide emotional support and encouragement. They can offer a listening ear, help you process your fears and anxieties, and remind you of your strengths and capabilities. Sharing your goals and challenges with loved ones can help alleviate feelings of isolation and provide a sense of security. Their belief in your abilities can boost your confidence and reinforce your commitment to taking risks.

4. **Professional Support**: Sometimes, seeking support from professionals such as coaches, therapists, or counselors can be beneficial. These professionals are trained to help you develop strategies for managing fear, building resilience, and achieving your goals. They can provide objective perspectives, help you identify and

address underlying issues, and offer techniques for personal growth and development.
5. **Building a Support Network**: Actively building a support network involves reaching out to individuals who can offer guidance, encouragement, and accountability. Attend networking events, join professional organizations, and participate in online communities related to your interests. Be proactive in seeking out relationships that can provide mutual support and growth. Remember that building a support network is a two-way street; be willing to offer your support and encouragement to others as well.
6. **Communicating Your Needs**: Clearly communicate your needs and goals to your support network. Let them know how they can best support you, whether it's through providing feedback, offering resources, or simply being there to listen. Open and honest communication can strengthen your relationships and ensure that you receive the support you need.

In conclusion, seeking support from mentors, peers, loved ones, and professionals is a crucial step in overcoming fear and achieving your goals. A strong support network provides valuable guidance, reassurance, and motivation, helping you navigate challenges and stay focused on your path. By surrounding yourself with supportive individuals, you can build the confidence and resilience needed to take bold risks and pursue your dreams.

## Practice Resilience

Developing a resilient mindset is crucial for overcoming fear and achieving long-term success. Resilience is the ability to bounce back from setbacks, adapt to change, and keep moving forward despite difficulties. By embracing failures as learning opportunities and reflecting on past experiences where you overcame challenges, you can build the mental toughness needed to face future risks with confidence.

1. **Embrace Failures as Learning Opportunities**: Instead of viewing failures as negative outcomes, reframe them as valuable learning experiences. Each failure provides insights into what went wrong and what can be improved. Ask yourself what lessons you can take away from the experience and how you can apply those lessons to future endeavors. This shift in perspective helps you see failures not as endpoints, but as stepping stones on the path to success.
2. **Reflect on Past Experiences**: Take time to reflect on past challenges and how you overcame them. Consider the strategies you used, the support you received, and the personal strengths you demonstrated. By analyzing these experiences, you can identify patterns of resilience and understand what works best for you. This reflection reinforces your ability to handle adversity and builds confidence in your capacity to navigate future obstacles.
3. **Cultivate a Growth Mindset**: A growth mindset is the belief that abilities and intelligence can be developed through effort, learning, and perseverance. Embracing this mindset encourages you to see challenges as opportunities to grow

rather than threats to your success. Focus on the process of learning and improvement rather than solely on the outcome. This approach fosters resilience by promoting a proactive attitude toward overcoming difficulties.
4. **Set Realistic Expectations**: Understand that setbacks and failures are a natural part of any journey. By setting realistic expectations, you can prepare yourself mentally for the inevitable ups and downs. Accept that progress may be slow and that achieving your goals will require persistence and determination. Managing your expectations helps prevent discouragement and keeps you motivated to continue pushing forward.
5. **Develop Coping Strategies**: Identify and practice coping strategies that help you manage stress and maintain a positive outlook during challenging times. Techniques such as mindfulness, meditation, deep breathing exercises, and physical activity can reduce anxiety and improve emotional resilience. Experiment with different strategies to find what works best for you and incorporate them into your daily routine.
6. **Build a Support System**: Surround yourself with supportive individuals who encourage and believe in you. A strong support system can provide emotional reassurance, practical advice, and a sense of belonging. Lean on your support network during difficult times and allow them to help you regain perspective and motivation.
7. **Maintain a Positive Outlook**: Cultivate a positive outlook by focusing on your strengths and achievements. Celebrate small victories and acknowledge your progress, no matter how minor it

may seem. Maintaining a positive attitude helps you stay resilient in the face of adversity and reinforces your belief in your ability to succeed.
8. **Take Action**: Resilience is built through action. Confronting challenges head-on and taking steps toward your goals, even in the face of fear, strengthens your resilience. Each small action you take reinforces your ability to handle adversity and builds momentum toward achieving your larger objectives.

In conclusion, practicing resilience involves embracing failures as learning opportunities, reflecting on past experiences, and developing strategies to cope with challenges. By cultivating a resilient mindset, you can navigate setbacks with confidence and perseverance, ultimately achieving your goals and realizing your full potential. Resilience is not about avoiding difficulties but about facing them with courage and determination, knowing that each challenge is an opportunity to grow stronger and wiser.

## Take Action

Sometimes, the best way to overcome fear is to take action despite it. Action dispels doubt and builds momentum, gradually transforming fear into confidence. By starting small and incrementally increasing the level of risk, you can build the courage and resilience needed to tackle more significant challenges over time.

1. **Start Small**: Begin by taking small, manageable steps toward your goal. These initial actions should be achievable and within your comfort zone, yet still require you to confront your fears. For example, if

you're afraid of public speaking, start by speaking in front of a small group of friends or colleagues. Small successes in these low-stakes situations can boost your confidence and prepare you for larger challenges.
2. **Set Incremental Goals**: Break down your larger goal into smaller, actionable milestones. Each milestone should represent a slight increase in risk or difficulty, allowing you to build confidence gradually. Celebrate each achievement, no matter how minor, as it signifies progress and reinforces your ability to take on more significant challenges.
3. **Embrace the Discomfort**: Understand that fear and discomfort are natural parts of the growth process. When you take action despite fear, you train your mind to become more comfortable with uncertainty and risk. Embrace the discomfort as a sign that you are pushing your boundaries and moving forward.
4. **Focus on the Present**: Concentrate on the task at hand rather than worrying about future outcomes. By staying present and focused on what you can control, you can reduce anxiety and increase your effectiveness. Mindfulness techniques, such as deep breathing and meditation, can help you stay grounded and centered.
5. **Learn from Each Experience**: After taking action, reflect on what you learned from the experience. Identify what went well, what challenges you faced, and how you can improve next time. Each action provides valuable feedback that can inform your future decisions and actions.
6. **Build a Routine**: Incorporate risk-taking into your daily routine. Consistency is key to building

confidence and overcoming fear. By making risk-taking a regular part of your life, you desensitize yourself to fear and make it easier to tackle larger challenges over time.
7. **Seek Accountability**: Share your goals and progress with a trusted friend, mentor, or accountability partner. Regular check-ins can provide motivation, encouragement, and constructive feedback. Knowing that someone else is aware of your efforts can also increase your commitment to taking action.
8. **Visualize Success**: Before taking action, visualize yourself successfully completing the task. Positive visualization can reduce anxiety and increase your confidence by mentally rehearsing success. Imagine how you will feel and the benefits you will gain from taking action.
9. **Accept Imperfection**: Understand that taking action does not require perfection. Mistakes and setbacks are part of the learning process. Be kind to yourself and recognize that each step, regardless of the outcome, is progress toward overcoming your fears.
10. **Adapt and Adjust**: Be flexible and willing to adjust your approach as needed. If a particular action doesn't yield the desired results, learn from it and try a different strategy. Adaptability is crucial to overcoming fear and achieving long-term success.

In conclusion, taking action is a powerful way to overcome fear and build confidence. By starting small, setting incremental goals, and embracing discomfort, you can gradually increase your tolerance for risk and achieve your larger objectives. Remember that each step, no matter how small, brings you closer to your goals and reinforces your ability to confront and conquer fear.

## Real-Life Stories of Individuals Who Conquered Their Fears

Real-life stories can provide powerful inspiration and demonstrate that overcoming fear is possible. Here are a few examples:

- **J.K. Rowling**
- Before becoming one of the most successful authors in the world, J.K. Rowling faced numerous rejections from publishers. Her journey to literary fame was marked by significant challenges, financial struggles, and moments of doubt. Yet, it was her persistence and determination to share her story that eventually led to the creation of the beloved Harry Potter series, inspiring millions worldwide.
- In the early 1990s, Rowling was a single mother living on welfare in Edinburgh, Scotland. She had conceived the idea for Harry Potter during a delayed train ride and spent the subsequent years writing the first book, often in cafes while her daughter slept beside her. Despite the personal hardships she faced, Rowling poured her creativity and passion into her manuscript, driven by a deep belief in her story.
- When she completed the manuscript for "Harry Potter and the Philosopher's Stone," Rowling began submitting it to literary agents and publishers. The road to publication was anything but smooth. She received rejection letter after

rejection letter, with many publishers doubting the commercial viability of a children's book about a young wizard. These rejections could have easily discouraged her, but Rowling's resilience kept her going. She believed in the magic of her story and was determined to find someone who would share that belief.

- Finally, after twelve rejections, Bloomsbury Publishing decided to take a chance on her book. Even then, Rowling was advised to get a day job, as she was told that she was unlikely to make much money from writing children's books. Despite these discouraging words, she continued to write, and the first Harry Potter book was published in 1997.
- The rest, as they say, is history. The Harry Potter series became a global phenomenon, selling over 500 million copies worldwide and being translated into more than 80 languages. The books have been adapted into highly successful films, and the franchise has expanded to include plays, theme parks, and a vast array of merchandise. Rowling's story is not just one of literary success but also one of perseverance, resilience, and the power of believing in oneself.
- J.K. Rowling's journey from a struggling single mother to a world-renowned author serves as a powerful example of how persistence and determination can lead to extraordinary success. Her story encourages us to keep pushing forward, even in the face of rejection and adversity. It reminds us that failure is not the end but a part of the journey toward achieving our dreams. By embracing resilience and maintaining faith in our

abilities, we too can overcome obstacles and realize our full potential.

- **Elon Musk**
- Known for his ambitious ventures, Elon Musk has faced multiple failures and setbacks throughout his career. His journey is a testament to the power of resilience and the ability to confront and overcome fear. From the early struggles of SpaceX to the near-collapse of Tesla, Musk's determination and vision have driven him to achieve groundbreaking successes in technology and space exploration.
- Elon Musk's entrepreneurial journey began with Zip2, a software company he co-founded with his brother. After selling Zip2, Musk founded X.com, which later became PayPal. Despite these early successes, Musk's true test of resilience came with his subsequent ventures: SpaceX and Tesla.
- In 2002, Musk founded SpaceX with the ambitious goal of reducing space transportation costs and making space exploration accessible. The initial years were fraught with challenges. The first three launches of the Falcon 1 rocket ended in failure, nearly bankrupting the company. Each failure brought immense pressure and scrutiny, and many doubted whether SpaceX could succeed. However, Musk's unwavering belief in his vision kept him and his team pushing forward. In 2008, the fourth launch of the Falcon 1 was successful, making SpaceX the first privately funded company to send a liquid-fueled rocket into orbit. This success was a pivotal moment, securing a NASA contract and setting the stage for future achievements.
- Around the same time, Musk was also facing significant challenges with Tesla, the electric car

company he co-founded in 2003. Tesla's early years were marked by production delays, technical issues, and financial difficulties. By 2008, the company was on the brink of collapse, and Musk had to make difficult decisions, including investing his personal fortune to keep Tesla afloat. Despite these hurdles, Musk's commitment to his vision of sustainable energy and electric vehicles never wavered. Through relentless effort and innovation, Tesla overcame its challenges and eventually became a leader in the electric vehicle industry. Today, Tesla is not only financially successful but has also played a crucial role in advancing the adoption of electric vehicles globally.

- Musk's ventures did not stop there. He continued to push the boundaries with projects like SolarCity, Neuralink, and The Boring Company, each addressing significant challenges in their respective fields. His ability to confront fear and persist through setbacks has been a driving force behind these endeavors.
- Elon Musk's story illustrates that failure and setbacks are inevitable parts of the entrepreneurial journey. His ability to confront these challenges head-on and learn from them has been crucial to his success. Musk's experience teaches us that resilience, coupled with a clear vision and unwavering determination, can lead to extraordinary achievements. By embracing failure as a learning opportunity and persisting through adversity, we can overcome obstacles and make significant strides toward our goals..
- **Oprah Winfrey**

- Overcoming a challenging childhood marked by poverty and abuse, Oprah Winfrey faced significant obstacles in her path to success. Her resilience and refusal to be defined by her past enabled her to become a media mogul and influential figure, inspiring countless individuals worldwide.
- Oprah was born in rural Mississippi to a teenage single mother. She experienced extreme hardship and trauma during her early years, including abuse and neglect. Despite these adversities, Oprah demonstrated remarkable resilience and a strong desire for a better life. She found solace and inspiration in education, which became her refuge and pathway to escape her difficult circumstances.
- At the age of 14, Oprah moved to Nashville to live with her father, Vernon Winfrey, who provided a more stable and supportive environment. Her father emphasized the importance of education and hard work, values that Oprah embraced wholeheartedly. She excelled academically and earned a scholarship to Tennessee State University, where she studied communication.
- Oprah's career in media began while she was still in high school, working as a part-time news reporter for a local radio station. Her natural talent and charisma quickly became evident, leading to opportunities in television. Oprah faced numerous challenges and setbacks in the male-dominated media industry, but her determination and resilience saw her through.
- In 1984, Oprah became the host of a struggling morning talk show in Chicago called "AM Chicago." Through her authentic and empathetic interviewing style, she transformed the show into a ratings

success, eventually renaming it "The Oprah Winfrey Show." Her show tackled a wide range of topics, including social issues, personal development, and health, resonating deeply with audiences. Oprah's ability to connect with people on a profound level made her a beloved and trusted figure.

- Oprah's influence extended beyond television. She launched her own production company, Harpo Productions, gaining control over her content and brand. This move allowed her to produce impactful projects such as "The Oprah Winfrey Network" (OWN), "O, The Oprah Magazine," and numerous films and documentaries. Her book club selections became cultural phenomena, boosting the careers of many authors and encouraging millions to read.
- Oprah's philanthropy and advocacy work further exemplify her commitment to making a positive impact. She has donated millions to educational initiatives, disaster relief, and other charitable causes. Her leadership and dedication to empowering others have earned her numerous accolades and honors, solidifying her legacy as a transformative figure.
- Oprah Winfrey's journey from a challenging childhood to becoming a media mogul and influential leader demonstrates the power of resilience and determination. Her story inspires us to rise above our circumstances, embrace our strengths, and pursue our dreams with unwavering resolve. Oprah's life teaches us that we can overcome even the most formidable obstacles through resilience, self-belief, and a commitment to making a difference in the world.

# Exercises to Help Readers Face and Mitigate Their Own Fears

To help you face and mitigate your fears, here are some practical exercises:

## Fear Inventory

Creating a fear inventory is a practical exercise that can help you gain perspective on your fears related to risk-taking and reduce the anxiety associated with them. By systematically identifying your fears and considering various outcomes, you can demystify your anxieties and develop a more balanced view of potential risks.

1. **Make a List of Your Fears**: Start by writing down all the fears you have related to taking risks. These might include fears about failure, rejection, financial loss, judgment from others, or personal disappointment. Be honest and thorough in listing every fear that comes to mind, no matter how minor or irrational it may seem.
2. **For Each Fear, Write Down the Worst-Case Scenario**: Next to each fear, describe the worst possible outcome if that fear were to come true. This step is crucial because it allows you to confront your fears head-on. By clearly defining the worst-case scenario, you can start to understand the extent of your fear and see it for what it truly is. Often, the worst-case scenario is not as catastrophic as we imagine.
    - **Example Fear**: Fear of starting a new business

- **Worst-Case Scenario**: The business fails, leading to financial loss, debt, and a damaged reputation.
3. **Write Down the Best-Case Scenario**: Now, consider the best possible outcome if everything goes well. This step helps you focus on the positive potential and the rewards that can come from taking risks. It serves as a reminder of what you stand to gain if you succeed.
    - **Example Fear**: Fear of starting a new business
    - **Best-Case Scenario**: The business thrives, providing financial stability, personal fulfillment, and recognition as a successful entrepreneur.
4. **Write Down the Most Likely Outcome**: Finally, assess the most realistic and probable outcome. This outcome usually lies somewhere between the worst-case and best-case scenarios. By evaluating the most likely outcome, you can ground your expectations in reality and reduce exaggerated fears.
    - **Example Fear**: Fear of starting a new business
    - **Most Likely Outcome**: The business faces initial challenges and requires adjustments but eventually finds a stable customer base and grows steadily over time.
5. **Analyze Your Fear Inventory**: Review your list and the various scenarios you've outlined. This process can help you gain a more balanced perspective on your fears. You'll likely find that the worst-case scenarios are less probable and less devastating than you initially thought, while the

best-case scenarios highlight the potential rewards of taking risks.
6. **Develop Action Plans**: For each fear, create an action plan to mitigate potential risks and enhance the likelihood of positive outcomes. Consider steps you can take to prepare for challenges, such as acquiring new skills, seeking advice from experts, or building a financial safety net. Having a plan in place can further reduce anxiety and increase your confidence in taking risks.
7. **Revisit Your Fear Inventory Regularly**: Fear inventories are not one-time exercises. Regularly revisiting and updating your list can help you stay aware of your evolving fears and continuously refine your strategies for managing them. As you gain more experience and confidence, you'll likely find that some fears diminish or disappear altogether.

By completing a fear inventory, you can confront your fears directly, gain a clearer understanding of potential outcomes, and develop strategies to manage risks effectively. This exercise empowers you to move forward with greater confidence and resilience, transforming fear into a manageable and constructive part of your risk-taking journey.

## Exposure Therapy

Exposure therapy is a powerful technique for overcoming fear by gradually exposing yourself to situations that trigger your anxiety. This method helps desensitize you to your fears, making them more manageable over time. By starting with low-risk scenarios and slowly increasing the level of risk as you become more comfortable, you can build confidence and resilience in facing your fears.

1. **Identify Your Fears**: Begin by clearly identifying the specific situations or activities that trigger your fears. These could range from public speaking and networking to taking financial risks or making significant life changes. Knowing exactly what you're afraid of will help you create a targeted and effective exposure plan.
2. **Create a Hierarchy of Fear**: Once you've identified your fears, arrange them in a hierarchy from least to most intimidating. This list should include a variety of scenarios, starting with low-risk situations that cause mild discomfort and progressing to high-risk situations that trigger intense fear. The goal is to gradually work your way up the hierarchy, gaining confidence and reducing anxiety with each step.
    - **Example Hierarchy for Public Speaking Fear**:
        - Practice speaking in front of a mirror.
        - Record a video of yourself giving a short speech and watch it.
        - Practice speaking in front of a close friend or family member.
        - Participate in a small group discussion.
        - Give a short presentation to a small, supportive group.
        - Speak at a larger, informal gathering.
        - Deliver a formal presentation to a larger audience.

3. **Start with Low-Risk Scenarios**: Begin your exposure therapy with the least intimidating situation on your hierarchy. The key is to start with something that causes mild discomfort but is still manageable. By successfully facing these low-risk scenarios, you can build a foundation of confidence and gradually reduce your fear.
4. **Gradually Increase the Level of Risk**: As you become more comfortable with each scenario, slowly move up your hierarchy to more challenging situations. Take your time with each step, ensuring you feel reasonably comfortable before progressing to the next level. This gradual approach helps prevent overwhelming anxiety and reinforces positive experiences.
5. **Practice Regularly**: Consistency is crucial for the success of exposure therapy. Regular practice helps reinforce your progress and further desensitizes you to your fears. Schedule regular sessions to expose yourself to the situations on your hierarchy, and make it a routine part of your efforts to overcome fear.
6. **Use Relaxation Techniques**: Incorporate relaxation techniques, such as deep breathing, mindfulness, or visualization, into your exposure therapy. These techniques can help you manage anxiety during exposure sessions and create a sense of calm and control.
7. **Reflect on Your Progress**: After each exposure session, take time to reflect on your experience. Note how you felt before, during, and after the exposure, and acknowledge any progress you made. Even small successes are significant and

should be celebrated as steps toward overcoming your fear.
8. **Seek Support**: Having a support system can be beneficial during exposure therapy. Share your goals and progress with a trusted friend, family member, or mentor who can provide encouragement and feedback. They can also help hold you accountable and motivate you to keep moving forward.
9. **Adjust Your Plan as Needed**: Be flexible and willing to adjust your exposure plan based on your experiences. If a particular step feels too overwhelming, break it down into smaller, more manageable tasks. Conversely, if you find a step easier than expected, you might move to the next level more quickly.

By gradually exposing yourself to situations that trigger your fears, you can desensitize yourself to those fears and build the confidence needed to face them head-on. Exposure therapy allows you to confront anxiety in a controlled and systematic way, transforming fearful situations into opportunities for growth and empowerment. With patience and persistence, you can overcome your fears and unlock your full potential.

## Mindfulness and Meditation

Practicing mindfulness and meditation techniques can be highly effective for managing anxiety and developing a more balanced approach to fear. These practices help you stay present and calm, allowing you to observe your thoughts and feelings without judgment. By incorporating mindfulness and meditation into your daily routine, you can reduce stress, enhance emotional resilience, and gain greater control over your fears.

1. **Understanding Mindfulness**: Mindfulness is the practice of paying attention to the present moment with an open and non-judgmental attitude. It involves being fully aware of your thoughts, emotions, bodily sensations, and surroundings. By focusing on the here and now, mindfulness helps you break free from the cycle of worrying about the past or future, which often fuels anxiety and fear.
2. **Basic Mindfulness Techniques**:
    - **Breath Awareness**: One of the simplest and most effective mindfulness techniques is breath awareness. Sit or lie down in a comfortable position, close your eyes, and focus on your breath. Notice the sensation of the air entering and leaving your nostrils, the rise and fall of your chest, and the rhythm of your breathing. Whenever your mind wanders, gently bring your focus back to your breath.
    - **Body Scan**: This technique involves paying attention to different parts of your body, one at a time. Starting from your toes and moving up to your head, notice any sensations, tension, or discomfort without trying to change anything. The body scan helps you become more aware of physical sensations and release any tension you might be holding.
    - **Mindful Observation**: Choose an object, such as a flower or a piece of fruit, and observe it closely. Notice its color, texture,

shape, and any other details. This practice helps you develop a habit of focusing on the present moment and appreciating the world around you.
3. **Understanding Meditation**: Meditation is a practice that involves focusing the mind to achieve a state of relaxation and mental clarity. There are various forms of meditation, each with its own techniques and benefits. Regular meditation can help reduce stress, improve concentration, and enhance emotional well-being.
4. **Basic Meditation Techniques**:
    - **Guided Meditation**: In guided meditation, a teacher or recording leads you through a series of visualizations and instructions. This type of meditation is helpful for beginners as it provides structure and guidance.
    - **Mantra Meditation**: This technique involves repeating a word or phrase (mantra) to focus the mind. The repetition of the mantra helps drown out distracting thoughts and induces a state of deep relaxation. Choose a mantra that resonates with you, such as "peace" or "calm," and repeat it silently or aloud.
    - **Loving-Kindness Meditation**: Also known as Metta meditation, this practice involves focusing on developing feelings of compassion and love for yourself and others. Start by silently repeating phrases such as "May I be happy, may I be healthy, may I be safe," and gradually extend these

wishes to loved ones, acquaintances, and even those with whom you have difficulties.
5. **Incorporating Mindfulness and Meditation into Daily Life**: To experience the full benefits of mindfulness and meditation, integrate these practices into your daily routine. Start with just a few minutes each day and gradually increase the duration as you become more comfortable. Find a quiet space where you can practice without distractions, and make it a regular part of your schedule.
6. **Managing Anxiety with Mindfulness and Meditation**: When faced with fear or anxiety, use mindfulness and meditation to center yourself. Practice deep breathing to calm your nervous system, and bring your focus to the present moment. By observing your thoughts and emotions without judgment, you can create a sense of distance from your fears and reduce their intensity.
7. **Developing a Balanced Approach to Fear**: Mindfulness and meditation help you develop a balanced approach to fear by fostering self-awareness and emotional regulation. By regularly practicing these techniques, you can cultivate a mindset that is better equipped to handle stress and uncertainty. This balanced perspective allows you to respond to fear with clarity and calmness, rather than reacting impulsively.

In conclusion, mindfulness and meditation are powerful tools for managing anxiety and developing a more balanced approach to fear. By staying present and calm, you can observe your thoughts and emotions without judgment, reducing their hold on you. Incorporate these practices into your daily routine to enhance your emotional resilience, gain greater control over your fears, and navigate life's challenges with confidence and ease.

## Journaling

Keeping a journal to document your experiences with fear and risk is a powerful tool for self-reflection and personal growth. Journaling helps you process and understand your fears, track your progress, and gain valuable insights into your journey. By regularly writing about your thoughts and emotions, you can develop a deeper awareness of your patterns, challenges, and successes.

1. **Documenting Experiences**: Use your journal to record specific instances where you faced fear and took risks. Write about the situation, your initial feelings, the actions you took, and the outcomes. This detailed documentation allows you to see patterns in how you respond to fear and identify areas for improvement.
    - **Example Entry**: "Today, I faced my fear of public speaking by giving a short presentation at work. I felt extremely nervous beforehand, but I practiced deep breathing to calm myself. During the presentation, I stumbled over a few words but managed to complete it. My colleagues were supportive, and I received positive feedback."
2. **Reflecting on Progress**: Regularly review your journal entries to reflect on your progress. Look for evidence of growth, such as increased confidence, improved coping strategies, or successful

outcomes. Acknowledge and celebrate these achievements, no matter how small they may seem. Recognizing your progress reinforces positive behavior and motivates you to continue taking risks.
    - **Reflection Example**: "Looking back at my entries from the past month, I've noticed that my anxiety before presentations has decreased. I'm becoming more comfortable speaking in front of others, and my preparation techniques are proving effective."
3. **Analyzing Setbacks**: Write about any setbacks or challenges you encounter. Reflect on what went wrong, how you felt, and what you can learn from the experience. Identifying the root causes of setbacks and developing strategies to address them can help you build resilience and prevent similar issues in the future.
    - **Setback Analysis**: "Last week, I experienced a setback when I hesitated to pitch my idea during a meeting. My fear of rejection held me back. I realized that I need to work on building my confidence and preparing better for such opportunities."
4. **Understanding Your Fears**: Use your journal to explore the underlying reasons for your fears. Ask yourself questions like, "What am I truly afraid of?" and "Why does this fear hold so much power over me?" Writing about your fears can help you uncover deeper insights and understand the sources of your anxiety.
    - **Fear Exploration**: "I'm afraid of rejection because I associate it with personal failure. I

need to remind myself that rejection is not a reflection of my worth but a part of the process."

5. **Setting Goals and Intentions**: Use your journal to set specific goals and intentions related to overcoming fear and taking risks. Write down actionable steps you plan to take and timelines for achieving them. Revisiting these goals regularly can keep you focused and accountable.
    - **Goal Setting**: "My goal for the next month is to speak up at least once in every team meeting. I'll prepare talking points in advance to feel more confident."

6. **Practicing Gratitude**: Incorporate gratitude into your journaling practice by writing about the positive aspects of your experiences. Focus on what you are grateful for, such as the support you receive from others, your personal strengths, or the lessons you've learned. Gratitude can shift your perspective and foster a positive mindset.
    - **Gratitude Entry**: "I'm grateful for my supportive colleagues who encourage me to speak up. Their positive feedback boosts my confidence and helps me overcome my fear of public speaking."

7. **Reviewing and Revising**: Periodically review your journal to assess your overall progress and adjust your strategies as needed. Use your reflections to refine your approach to risk-taking and fear management. Continuous improvement is key to personal growth.
    - **Review Example**: "After reviewing my journal, I've decided to seek additional

training in public speaking. This will help me build more skills and confidence."

In conclusion, journaling is an effective way to document your experiences with fear and risk, reflect on your progress, analyze setbacks, and set goals. By regularly writing about your thoughts and emotions, you can gain a deeper understanding of your fears and develop strategies to overcome them. Journaling fosters self-awareness, resilience, and personal growth, empowering you to take bold actions and achieve your goals.

## Affirmations

Use positive affirmations to counter negative thoughts. Repeat empowering statements to yourself, such as "I am capable of overcoming challenges" or "I embrace uncertainty as a path to growth." Affirmations are a powerful tool for reshaping your mindset and reinforcing a positive self-image. By consistently affirming your strengths and potential, you can build confidence and resilience, making it easier to face fears and take risks.

1. **Understanding Affirmations**: Affirmations are short, positive statements that you repeat to yourself to challenge and overcome negative thoughts and self-doubt. They work by reinforcing positive beliefs and attitudes, helping you to cultivate a more optimistic and empowering mindset.
2. **Choosing Affirmations**: Select affirmations that resonate with you and address your specific fears and goals. The statements should be positive, present-tense, and focus on what you want to

achieve or believe. Examples of effective affirmations include:
    - "I am confident and capable in all that I do."
    - "I have the strength and courage to face my fears."
    - "I am open to new opportunities and embrace change with ease."
    - "I trust in my abilities and make wise decisions."
3. **Incorporating Affirmations into Your Routine**: Make affirmations a regular part of your daily routine. Repeat them in the morning to set a positive tone for the day, during moments of stress or doubt, and before important events or challenges. The key is to be consistent and genuine in your repetition.
4. **Using Visual and Auditory Cues**: Enhance the effectiveness of affirmations by incorporating visual and auditory cues. Write your affirmations on sticky notes and place them where you will see them frequently, such as on your mirror, desk, or refrigerator. You can also record yourself saying the affirmations and listen to the playback during your commute or while relaxing.
5. **Combining Affirmations with Visualization**: Pair your affirmations with visualization techniques to strengthen their impact. As you repeat each affirmation, close your eyes and visualize yourself embodying the qualities and achieving the outcomes you are affirming. Imagine the feelings of confidence, success, and fulfillment that come with these achievements.
6. **Believing in Your Affirmations**: The effectiveness of affirmations depends on your belief in them. If

you find it difficult to believe in a particular affirmation, start with a statement that feels more attainable and gradually build up to stronger affirmations. For example, if "I am confident" feels too far from your current experience, begin with "I am becoming more confident every day."

7. **Affirmations in Challenging Moments**: Use affirmations as a tool to counteract negative thoughts and self-doubt in challenging moments. When you catch yourself thinking negatively or feeling overwhelmed, pause and repeat your affirmations. This practice helps to interrupt the cycle of negative thinking and shift your focus to a more positive and empowering mindset.

8. **Tracking Your Progress**: Keep track of your progress with affirmations by noting any changes in your thoughts, feelings, and behaviors. Reflect on how affirmations have helped you face fears, take risks, and achieve your goals. Celebrate your successes and adjust your affirmations as needed to continue supporting your growth.

In conclusion, affirmations are a simple yet powerful tool for countering negative thoughts and building a positive mindset. By regularly repeating empowering statements, you can strengthen your confidence, resilience, and willingness to take risks. Incorporate affirmations into your daily routine, combine them with visualization, and believe in their potential to transform your mindset and help you achieve your goals.

By understanding and addressing the fears that hold us back, we can build the confidence needed to take crucial risks and pursue our goals with determination and resilience.

# Chapter 3

# Calculated Risks

## Understanding the Difference Between Reckless and Calculated Risks

Calculated risks are strategic decisions made after careful consideration of potential outcomes, benefits, and drawbacks. Unlike reckless risks, which are taken without adequate thought or planning, calculated risks involve a thorough analysis and a structured approach to decision-making. Understanding this distinction is crucial for making informed choices that maximize potential rewards while minimizing possible downsides.

Reckless risks often stem from impulsive actions, lack of information, or emotional responses. These risks tend to ignore potential negative consequences and are more likely to lead to failure. For example, investing a large sum of money in a business venture without conducting proper market research is a reckless risk. The decision is based on a gut feeling or a desire for quick gains, without understanding the market dynamics or the feasibility of the business model. Such actions can result in significant losses and missed opportunities for learning and growth.

On the other hand, calculated risks involve deliberate planning, informed judgment, and a balanced assessment of both positive and negative outcomes. This approach ensures that all potential scenarios are considered and that decisions are based on data and strategic thinking rather than emotion. For instance, before launching a new product, a company might conduct extensive market research, analyze consumer trends, and develop a detailed business plan. By doing so, they can anticipate potential challenges and prepare strategies to address them, increasing the likelihood of a successful launch.

By understanding and embracing calculated risks, you can make decisions that are more likely to lead to successful outcomes. Here are some key characteristics that differentiate calculated risks from reckless ones:

1. **Research and Information Gathering**: Calculated risks are grounded in thorough research and data collection. This process involves gathering relevant information, analyzing market trends, consulting experts, and considering historical data. Armed with this knowledge, you can make more informed

decisions that are based on factual evidence rather than assumptions.
2. **Strategic Planning**: A calculated risk involves careful planning and the development of a detailed strategy. This includes setting clear objectives, outlining the steps needed to achieve them, and identifying potential obstacles and solutions. Strategic planning helps ensure that all aspects of the decision are considered and that there is a roadmap for implementation.
3. **Risk Assessment**: Calculated risks require a comprehensive assessment of potential outcomes, both positive and negative. This involves evaluating the likelihood of success, the potential impact of failure, and the resources required. By assessing these factors, you can determine whether the potential benefits justify the risks involved.
4. **Contingency Planning**: Part of taking a calculated risk is preparing for possible setbacks. This involves developing contingency plans and alternative strategies to address unforeseen challenges. Having a backup plan in place can mitigate the impact of adverse outcomes and ensure that you are better prepared to navigate difficulties.
5. **Emotional Regulation**: Calculated risks are taken with a clear and rational mindset, free from emotional bias. While intuition can play a role in decision-making, it is important to balance it with logical reasoning and objective analysis. Managing emotions and staying focused on the facts can help prevent impulsive decisions that could lead to negative consequences.

6. **Regular Review and Adaptation**: Calculated risks involve ongoing evaluation and adjustment. This means regularly reviewing progress, assessing the effectiveness of the strategies employed, and making necessary changes based on new information. Continuous monitoring ensures that you stay on track and can adapt to changing circumstances.

In summary, the difference between reckless and calculated risks lies in the approach to decision-making. Reckless risks are taken without sufficient thought or planning, often driven by impulse or emotion. Calculated risks, on the other hand, involve careful consideration, informed judgment, and strategic planning. By understanding and embracing calculated risks, you can make decisions that are more likely to lead to successful outcomes, maximizing rewards while minimizing potential downsides.

## Tools and Frameworks for Assessing Risk

To take calculated risks effectively, it's essential to use tools and frameworks that help assess and manage uncertainty. Here are some key methods:

### SWOT Analysis

SWOT Analysis is a powerful framework used to evaluate the Strengths, Weaknesses, Opportunities, and Threats related to a decision. By identifying internal strengths and weaknesses, as well as external opportunities and threats, you can gain a comprehensive understanding of the potential risks and benefits. This balanced analysis helps you make more informed and strategic decisions.

## Strengths

Strengths are internal attributes and resources that support a successful outcome. These might include unique skills, strong financial resources, brand recognition, or a loyal customer base. Identifying strengths allows you to leverage these assets to maximize your chances of success.

- **Example**: A company considering the launch of a new product might identify its strong brand recognition as a key strength. This established reputation can facilitate market acceptance and customer trust, giving the new product a competitive edge.

## Weaknesses

Weaknesses are internal factors that could hinder progress or contribute to failure. These might include limited resources, gaps in expertise, poor infrastructure, or a weak market presence. Recognizing weaknesses is essential for addressing them proactively and minimizing their impact.

- **Example**: In the same product launch scenario, limited market research could be identified as a weakness. This lack of data may lead to misinformed decisions about product features, pricing, and target audience, increasing the risk of failure.

## Opportunities

Opportunities are external factors that could be leveraged for success. These might include market trends, economic conditions, technological advancements, or changes in consumer behavior. Identifying opportunities helps you to capitalize on favorable conditions and gain a competitive advantage.

- **Example**: Growing demand for eco-friendly products might be an opportunity for the new product. If the product aligns with this trend, the company can position it to attract environmentally conscious consumers, increasing its market potential.

**Threats**

Threats are external factors that could pose challenges or risks. These might include competition, regulatory changes, economic downturns, or shifts in consumer preferences. Recognizing threats allows you to develop strategies to mitigate their impact and safeguard against potential obstacles.

- **Example**: Strong competition from established brands could be a significant threat to the new product. Competitors with greater market share and resources might pose a challenge to gaining traction and achieving desired sales targets.

**Conducting a SWOT Analysis**

1. **Gather Information**: Collect relevant data about the internal and external environment. This can include financial reports, market research, customer feedback, and industry trends.

2. **Brainstorm**: Engage key stakeholders in a brainstorming session to identify strengths, weaknesses, opportunities, and threats. Encourage open discussion and diverse perspectives to ensure a comprehensive analysis.
3. **Categorize**: Organize the identified factors into the four SWOT categories. Be specific and objective in your assessment to ensure accuracy.
4. **Analyze**: Evaluate each category to understand its impact on the decision at hand. Consider how strengths can be leveraged, weaknesses can be mitigated, opportunities can be seized, and threats can be managed.
5. **Develop Strategies**: Use the insights gained from the SWOT analysis to formulate strategies that maximize strengths and opportunities while addressing weaknesses and threats. This strategic planning will help you make informed decisions and increase the likelihood of success.

### Example: SWOT Analysis for Launching a New Product

- **Strengths**: Strong brand recognition, loyal customer base, robust financial resources.
- **Weaknesses**: Limited market research, gaps in the product development team's expertise, insufficient production capacity.
- **Opportunities**: Growing demand for eco-friendly products, favorable economic conditions, advancements in sustainable technology.
- **Threats**: Strong competition from established brands, potential regulatory changes, economic uncertainty.

By conducting a SWOT analysis, you can gain a holistic view of the factors influencing your decision. This comprehensive understanding enables you to strategically navigate risks and capitalize on opportunities, ultimately leading to more successful outcomes.

## Cost-Benefit Analysis

Cost-benefit analysis is a valuable tool used to compare the costs and benefits of a particular action. By quantifying both the tangible and intangible factors, you can determine whether the potential rewards outweigh the risks. This systematic approach helps in making informed and rational decisions by highlighting the financial and non-financial implications of a given course of action.

### Conducting a Cost-Benefit Analysis

1. **Identify the Costs**: Begin by listing all the costs associated with the action. These costs can be direct or indirect, and may include initial investments, ongoing expenses, and potential hidden costs.
    - **Direct Costs**: These are easily quantifiable and directly linked to the action, such as equipment purchase, labor, materials, and licensing fees.
    - **Indirect Costs**: These are not as immediately obvious but still impact the overall cost, such as administrative expenses, training, and maintenance.
2. **Identify the Benefits**: Next, list all the potential benefits of the action. Benefits can also be direct or indirect, and may include financial gains, improved efficiency, market growth, and intangible benefits

such as enhanced reputation or employee satisfaction.
   - **Direct Benefits**: These are easily measurable, such as increased revenue, cost savings, and higher profit margins.
   - **Indirect Benefits**: These may include improved customer satisfaction, stronger brand loyalty, better employee morale, and long-term strategic advantages.
3. **Quantify the Costs and Benefits**: Assign monetary values to both the costs and benefits as accurately as possible. This step might involve estimating the financial impact of intangible factors, which can be challenging but is essential for a comprehensive analysis.
4. **Calculate the Net Benefit**: Subtract the total costs from the total benefits to determine the net benefit. A positive net benefit indicates that the benefits outweigh the costs, suggesting that the action is worthwhile. Conversely, a negative net benefit suggests that the costs exceed the benefits, indicating that the action may not be advisable.
5. **Analyze the Results**: Evaluate the net benefit in the context of your overall goals and risk tolerance. Consider not only the financial outcomes but also the strategic and long-term implications of the decision.

**Example: Cost-Benefit Analysis for Expanding a Business**

**Scenario**: A company is considering expanding its operations by opening a new branch in a different city. The decision requires a thorough cost-benefit analysis to ensure it is financially viable and aligns with the company's strategic goals.

- **Costs:**
  - **Direct Costs:**
    - Initial setup costs: $200,000 (construction, equipment, furniture)
    - Hiring and training new staff: $100,000
    - Marketing and advertising: $50,000
    - Additional inventory: $75,000
  - **Indirect Costs:**
    - Increased administrative overhead: $30,000
    - Travel and accommodation for management: $20,000
    - Ongoing maintenance and utilities: $25,000 per year
- **Benefits:**
  - **Direct Benefits:**
    - Estimated annual revenue increase: $500,000
    - Cost savings from economies of scale: $50,000
  - **Indirect Benefits:**
    - Increased market share in the new region
    - Enhanced brand visibility and reputation
    - Improved customer accessibility and convenience

**Quantification:**

- **Total Costs** (first year): $200,000 + $100,000 + $50,000 + $75,000 + $30,000 + $20,000 + $25,000 = $500,000
- **Total Benefits** (first year): $500,000 + $50,000 (direct) + qualitative value of market share, brand visibility, customer accessibility (estimated at $100,000 for analysis purposes) = $650,000

**Net Benefit**: $650,000 (benefits) - $500,000 (costs) = $150,000

**Analysis**:

- The net benefit of $150,000 indicates that the expansion is financially viable in the first year.
- The indirect benefits, while more challenging to quantify precisely, suggest long-term strategic advantages that could further justify the expansion.
- Given the positive net benefit and alignment with strategic goals, the company might decide to proceed with the expansion.

By conducting a cost-benefit analysis, you can make well-informed decisions that weigh the potential rewards against the associated risks. This analytical approach helps ensure that resources are allocated effectively and that actions taken align with your overall objectives and risk tolerance.

## Risk Matrix

A risk matrix is a valuable tool that helps prioritize risks based on their likelihood and impact. By categorizing risks into low, medium, and high levels, you can focus on managing the most critical risks while monitoring the less significant ones. This structured approach ensures that you allocate resources and attention effectively, addressing the risks that pose the greatest threat to your objectives.

## Understanding the Risk Matrix

A risk matrix typically consists of a grid with two axes: likelihood (probability of occurrence) and impact (consequence of occurrence). Each axis is divided into levels, usually low, medium, and high. Risks are plotted on the matrix based on their assessed likelihood and impact, providing a visual representation of their priority.

## Steps to Create and Use a Risk Matrix

1. **Identify Risks**: Begin by identifying all potential risks associated with your project or decision. These can include financial risks, operational risks, market risks, regulatory risks, and more.
2. **Assess Likelihood**: Evaluate the probability of each risk occurring. Assign a likelihood rating to each risk, such as:
    - Low: Unlikely to occur
    - Medium: Possible but not certain
    - High: Likely to occur
3. **Assess Impact**: Evaluate the potential impact of each risk if it were to occur. Assign an impact rating to each risk, such as:
    - Low: Minor consequences that can be easily managed
    - Medium: Moderate consequences that require some management effort
    - High: Significant consequences that could severely affect the project or decision

4. **Plot Risks on the Matrix**: Place each risk on the risk matrix based on its likelihood and impact ratings. The intersection of these two ratings will determine the risk's position on the matrix.
5. **Prioritize Risks**: Use the matrix to prioritize risks. High-impact, high-likelihood risks should receive immediate attention and resources, while low-impact, low-likelihood risks can be monitored with less urgency. Medium-level risks fall somewhere in between and should be managed accordingly.

**Example: Using a Risk Matrix to Assess Project Risks**

**Scenario**: A company is undertaking a large-scale IT project to upgrade its internal systems. The project manager uses a risk matrix to assess and prioritize potential risks.

1. **Identify Risks**:
    - Data breaches during migration
    - Delays due to vendor issues
    - Employee resistance to new system
    - Regulatory compliance changes
    - Cost overruns
2. **Assess Likelihood**:
    - Data breaches: Medium
    - Vendor issues: High
    - Employee resistance: Medium
    - Regulatory changes: Low
    - Cost overruns: Medium
3. **Assess Impact**:
    - Data breaches: High
    - Vendor issues: Medium
    - Employee resistance: Low

- Regulatory changes: High
- Cost overruns: Medium

**Prioritize Risks**:

- **High Impact, High Likelihood**: Data breaches (immediate attention)
- **High Impact, Low Likelihood**: Regulatory changes (monitoring)
- **Medium Impact, High Likelihood**: Vendor issues (close management)
- **Medium Impact, Medium Likelihood**: Cost overruns (regular oversight)
- **Low Impact, Medium Likelihood**: Employee resistance (minor management)

## Managing the Risks

- **Data Breaches**: Implement robust cybersecurity measures, conduct regular audits, and ensure compliance with data protection regulations.
- **Vendor Issues**: Maintain close communication with vendors, establish contingency plans, and have backup vendors ready if needed.
- **Cost Overruns**: Monitor budget closely, implement cost control measures, and regularly review financial performance.
- **Employee Resistance**: Provide training, communicate benefits of the new system, and involve employees in the transition process.
- **Regulatory Changes**: Stay informed about potential regulatory changes, consult with legal experts, and adjust project plans as necessary.

By using a risk matrix, you can visually and systematically prioritize risks, ensuring that the most critical risks are addressed first. This approach helps in efficiently managing resources and efforts, ultimately leading to more successful project outcomes.

## Scenario Planning

Scenario planning is a strategic tool that involves envisioning different scenarios and their potential outcomes. By considering best-case, worst-case, and most likely scenarios, you can prepare for various possibilities and develop contingency plans. This approach allows you to anticipate challenges, identify opportunities, and create flexible strategies that can adapt to changing circumstances.

### Steps to Conduct Scenario Planning

1. **Identify Key Factors**: Begin by identifying the key factors that could impact your decision or project. These might include market trends, economic conditions, regulatory changes, technological advancements, and competitive dynamics. Understanding these factors is crucial for developing relevant scenarios.
2. **Develop Scenarios**: Create a range of scenarios that reflect different possible futures. Typically, you should develop at least three scenarios: best-case, worst-case, and most likely. Each scenario should be detailed and consider how the key factors identified will influence outcomes.
    - **Best-Case Scenario**: This optimistic scenario assumes favorable conditions and successful outcomes. It is useful for

identifying potential opportunities and setting ambitious goals.
    - **Worst-Case Scenario**: This pessimistic scenario assumes unfavorable conditions and potential failures. It helps identify risks and prepare for adverse outcomes.
    - **Most Likely Scenario**: This scenario assumes moderate conditions and outcomes that are most probable. It serves as a baseline for planning and decision-making.
3. **Analyze Implications**: Evaluate the potential implications of each scenario. Consider the impact on resources, finances, operations, and strategic goals. This analysis helps you understand the consequences of different scenarios and prioritize actions accordingly.
4. **Develop Contingency Plans**: For each scenario, develop contingency plans that outline specific actions to take if that scenario occurs. These plans should include strategies for mitigating risks, capitalizing on opportunities, and adapting to changing conditions.
5. **Monitor and Adapt**: Scenario planning is an ongoing process. Continuously monitor relevant factors and update your scenarios and contingency plans as new information becomes available. This flexibility ensures that you remain prepared for any eventuality.

**Example: Scenario Planning for a New Market Entry**

**Scenario**: A company is considering entering a new international market. The decision requires thorough scenario planning to ensure preparedness for various market conditions.

1. **Identify Key Factors**:
    - Economic conditions in the target market
    - Regulatory environment and potential changes
    - Competitive landscape and existing market players
    - Consumer behavior and preferences
    - Currency exchange rates
2. **Develop Scenarios**:
    - **Best-Case Scenario**:
        - **Assumptions**: Strong economic growth, favorable regulatory environment, weak competition, high consumer demand, and stable currency exchange rates.
        - **Outcomes**: Rapid market penetration, high sales growth, strong brand establishment, and significant market share.
    - **Worst-Case Scenario**:
        - **Assumptions**: Economic recession, unfavorable regulatory changes, intense competition, low consumer demand, and volatile currency exchange rates.
        - **Outcomes**: Slow market penetration, low sales growth, high operational costs, and minimal market share.
    - **Most Likely Scenario**:

- **Assumptions**: Moderate economic growth, stable regulatory environment, moderate competition, steady consumer demand, and relatively stable currency exchange rates.
- **Outcomes**: Gradual market penetration, moderate sales growth, manageable operational costs, and reasonable market share.

3. **Analyze Implications**:
   - **Best-Case Scenario**: High revenue growth, opportunity to reinvest profits, potential for market leadership, and strong return on investment.
   - **Worst-Case Scenario**: Financial losses, need for cost-cutting measures, potential exit strategy, and reputation risk.
   - **Most Likely Scenario**: Steady revenue growth, balanced investment, gradual brand establishment, and sustainable market presence.

4. **Develop Contingency Plans**:
   - **Best-Case Scenario**:
     - Scale up production and distribution to meet high demand
     - Increase marketing efforts to capitalize on favorable conditions
     - Invest in market research to sustain growth
   - **Worst-Case Scenario**:
     - Implement cost control measures to manage financial losses

- Develop a flexible pricing strategy to attract price-sensitive consumers
- Establish an exit strategy to minimize losses if market conditions worsen
  - **Most Likely Scenario**:
    - Monitor economic and regulatory changes closely
    - Adjust marketing and sales strategies based on consumer feedback
    - Maintain a flexible budget to adapt to changing conditions

5. **Monitor and Adapt**:
   - Regularly review economic indicators, regulatory updates, and competitive actions
   - Update scenarios and contingency plans based on new data
   - Stay agile and ready to pivot strategies as needed

By using scenario planning, the company can better prepare for different market conditions and make informed decisions about entering the new market. This approach ensures that they are ready to navigate challenges, seize opportunities, and achieve their strategic objectives, regardless of how the market evolves.

## Case Studies of Successful Calculated Risks

Learning from real-life examples of successful calculated risks can provide valuable insights and inspiration. Here are a few notable case studies:

## Apple's Launch of the iPhone

In 2007, Apple took a calculated risk by entering the highly competitive mobile phone market with the iPhone. This decision involved significant challenges and uncertainties, but Apple's approach demonstrates how thorough market research, innovative technology, and a strong brand can mitigate risks and lead to groundbreaking successes.

### The Calculated Risk

Apple's entry into the mobile phone market was not an impulsive decision. It was a well-considered move that involved extensive market research and strategic planning. The company recognized the potential for innovation in a market dominated by established players like Nokia, Motorola, and BlackBerry. By identifying gaps and opportunities, Apple aimed to introduce a product that would redefine the user experience and set new standards in the industry.

### Market Research

Apple's market research was pivotal in shaping the iPhone's development. The company analyzed consumer needs and preferences, identifying a demand for a device that combined phone functionality with media capabilities and internet access. This research highlighted the limitations of existing mobile phones and the potential market for a more integrated, user-friendly device.

Key insights from Apple's market research included:

- Consumers' frustration with the complexity of existing smartphones.

- A growing desire for mobile internet access and multimedia capabilities.
- The potential for a touch-screen interface to enhance usability.

**Innovative Technology**

Leveraging its strengths in technology and design, Apple developed the iPhone with several groundbreaking features:

- **Multi-touch Screen**: The iPhone's intuitive touch-screen interface was a significant departure from the physical keyboards and styluses used by other smartphones. This innovation made the device more user-friendly and versatile.
- **Integrated Functions**: The iPhone combined a phone, iPod, and internet communicator in one device, offering seamless integration of communication, entertainment, and web browsing.
- **App Store**: While not part of the initial launch, the subsequent introduction of the App Store expanded the iPhone's capabilities, allowing users to download third-party applications and further enhancing the device's functionality.

**Strong Brand**

Apple's strong brand reputation played a crucial role in the iPhone's success. The company's history of innovation and quality products, such as the iPod and Mac computers, built consumer trust and anticipation for the new device. Apple's effective marketing campaigns also generated significant buzz and excitement, positioning the iPhone as a revolutionary product.

## Outcome

The iPhone revolutionized the mobile phone industry and became one of the most successful products in history. It set new standards for smartphone design and functionality, influencing competitors and shaping the future of mobile technology. The iPhone's success also solidified Apple's position as a leading technology company and contributed significantly to its financial growth.

## Lesson

Apple's launch of the iPhone illustrates that thorough market research and leveraging existing strengths can turn calculated risks into groundbreaking successes. By understanding consumer needs, innovating with cutting-edge technology, and capitalizing on a strong brand, Apple was able to navigate the competitive landscape and achieve unprecedented success.

This case study highlights the importance of:

- **Conducting Comprehensive Market Research**: Understanding the market and consumer needs is essential for identifying opportunities and mitigating risks.
- **Innovating with Purpose**: Leveraging technological strengths and designing products that offer real value to users can differentiate your offerings and drive success.
- **Building and Leveraging Brand Strength**: A strong brand reputation can generate consumer trust and excitement, facilitating market entry and adoption.

By applying these principles, businesses can make informed decisions and take calculated risks that have the potential to achieve transformative success.

## Netflix's Transition to Streaming

In the early 2000s, Netflix made a strategic decision to shift from a DVD rental service to a streaming platform. This transition involved significant investment and risk, but by leveraging technology trends and consumer behavior insights, Netflix transformed into a leading global entertainment service. This case study illustrates how adapting to technological advancements and consumer trends can create new growth opportunities.

### The Calculated Risk

Netflix's transition to streaming was a bold and calculated risk. At the time, the company was known for its DVD rental service, which allowed customers to rent movies online and receive them by mail. Despite its success, Netflix recognized that the future of entertainment was shifting towards digital delivery. The company saw an opportunity to capitalize on the growing demand for instant access to media content and decided to invest heavily in developing a streaming platform.

### Leveraging Technology Trends

The early 2000s saw rapid advancements in internet technology, including increased broadband speeds and improved video compression techniques. These technological developments made streaming video content more feasible and attractive to consumers. Netflix anticipated that these trends would continue to evolve, making streaming a more viable option for delivering entertainment.

Key technological factors considered by Netflix included:

- **Broadband Internet Penetration**: The increasing availability of high-speed internet connections made it possible for consumers to stream high-quality video content without significant buffering or interruptions.
- **Advancements in Compression Technology**: Improved video compression algorithms allowed for better quality streaming at lower bandwidths, making the experience more enjoyable for users.
- **Growth of Connected Devices**: The proliferation of devices capable of streaming video, such as smart TVs, gaming consoles, and smartphones, expanded the potential audience for streaming services.

### Understanding Consumer Behavior

Netflix's decision to transition to streaming was also driven by insights into changing consumer behavior. The company observed that consumers were increasingly seeking convenience and instant gratification in their entertainment choices. The traditional DVD rental model, which involved waiting for physical discs to arrive by mail, was becoming less appealing in an era where instant access to content was becoming the norm.

Key consumer behavior insights included:

- **Desire for Instant Access**: Consumers wanted immediate access to a wide range of content without the delays associated with physical media.
- **Preference for On-Demand Viewing**: The ability to watch content on-demand, at any time and on any device, was becoming increasingly important to viewers.
- **Shift Away from Physical Media**: There was a growing trend towards digital consumption of media, with consumers showing a preference for streaming and downloading content over purchasing or renting physical discs.

### Strategic Implementation

To successfully transition to a streaming platform, Netflix made several strategic moves:

- **Investment in Technology**: Netflix invested heavily in building a robust streaming infrastructure, including data centers and content delivery networks, to ensure a seamless streaming experience for users.
- **Content Licensing and Original Production**: Netflix secured licensing agreements with major studios to offer a wide selection of movies and TV shows on its platform. Additionally, the company began producing its own original content to differentiate itself from competitors and attract subscribers.
- **User Experience Optimization**: Netflix focused on creating an intuitive and user-friendly interface, making it easy for subscribers to discover and enjoy content. Personalized recommendations,

based on viewing history and preferences, enhanced the overall user experience.

## Outcome

Netflix's transition to streaming proved to be a transformative move. The company quickly gained a large subscriber base and established itself as a pioneer in the streaming industry. Today, Netflix is a global entertainment powerhouse, with millions of subscribers worldwide and a vast library of original and licensed content. The success of Netflix's streaming platform has also influenced the broader entertainment industry, prompting other companies to develop their own streaming services.

## Lesson

Netflix's transition to streaming demonstrates that adapting to technological advancements and consumer trends can create new growth opportunities. By anticipating changes in the market and leveraging technology and consumer insights, Netflix was able to reinvent its business model and achieve unprecedented success.

This case study highlights the importance of:

- **Staying Ahead of Technological Trends**: Keeping an eye on technological developments and understanding their potential impact on your industry can help you identify opportunities for innovation and growth.
- **Understanding Consumer Preferences**: Conducting thorough research on consumer behavior and preferences can provide valuable insights that inform strategic decisions.

- **Investing in Infrastructure and Content**: Building a strong technological foundation and offering high-quality content are critical to delivering a superior user experience and differentiating your service from competitors.

By applying these principles, businesses can navigate changing market dynamics and seize new opportunities for growth and success.

## Elon Musk and SpaceX

Elon Musk's decision to invest in SpaceX was a high-stakes gamble. The early years were marked by multiple failed rocket launches. However, through relentless innovation, strategic planning, and securing key partnerships, SpaceX succeeded in reducing space transportation costs and achieving historic milestones. This case study illustrates how persistence and innovation are critical in turning high-risk ventures into successful enterprises.

### The High-Stakes Gamble

In 2002, Elon Musk founded Space Exploration Technologies Corp. (SpaceX) with the ambitious goal of making space travel more affordable and eventually enabling human life on Mars. This venture was a high-stakes gamble because the space industry was dominated by well-established players like NASA and major aerospace companies, and space exploration was notoriously expensive and complex.

### Early Challenges and Failures

The early years of SpaceX were fraught with challenges and setbacks. The company faced technical difficulties, financial constraints, and skepticism from industry experts. The first three launches of SpaceX's Falcon 1 rocket ended in failure, putting immense pressure on Musk and his team. Each failure was a significant financial and emotional blow, bringing the company to the brink of bankruptcy.

Key challenges included:

- **Technical Failures**: The initial rocket launches failed due to a variety of technical issues, including engine failures and fuel leaks.
- **Financial Strain**: Repeated failures strained SpaceX's financial resources, as each launch represented a significant investment.
- **Industry Skepticism**: Many in the aerospace industry doubted SpaceX's ability to succeed, given the complexity and cost of space missions.

**Relentless Innovation**

Despite these setbacks, Musk and his team remained committed to their vision. They adopted a relentless approach to innovation, constantly iterating on their designs and learning from each failure. This commitment to continuous improvement was a cornerstone of SpaceX's eventual success.

Innovative strategies included:

- **Reusable Rockets**: One of SpaceX's most groundbreaking innovations was the development of reusable rocket technology. The Falcon 9

rocket's first stage could be recovered and reused, significantly reducing the cost of space missions.
- **Vertical Integration**: SpaceX adopted a vertically integrated approach, manufacturing many of its components in-house to reduce costs and improve quality control.
- **Rapid Prototyping**: The company embraced a culture of rapid prototyping and testing, allowing them to quickly identify and address issues.

### Strategic Planning and Partnerships

Strategic planning and key partnerships played a crucial role in SpaceX's success. Musk's ability to secure contracts and partnerships with government agencies and private companies provided the financial stability and credibility needed to continue operations.

Key strategic moves included:

- **NASA Contracts**: In 2006, SpaceX won a contract from NASA under the Commercial Orbital Transportation Services (COTS) program. This partnership provided critical funding and support, enabling SpaceX to develop its Falcon 9 rocket and Dragon spacecraft.
- **Commercial Launch Services**: SpaceX secured contracts with commercial customers for satellite launches, diversifying its revenue streams and demonstrating the reliability of its launch services.
- **Collaboration with International Space Agencies**: SpaceX partnered with international space agencies to expand its global reach and capabilities.

## Historic Milestones

SpaceX's persistence and innovation paid off with several historic milestones that revolutionized space travel:

- **First Successful Launch**: In 2008, SpaceX achieved its first successful launch with the Falcon 1 rocket, marking a turning point for the company.
- **Dragon's First Flight to ISS**: In 2012, SpaceX's Dragon spacecraft became the first commercial vehicle to dock with the International Space Station (ISS), demonstrating the viability of commercial space missions.
- **Reusable Rocket Landings**: SpaceX successfully landed the first stage of its Falcon 9 rocket in 2015, proving the feasibility of reusable rocket technology and significantly reducing launch costs.

## Lesson

Elon Musk and SpaceX's journey demonstrates that persistence and innovation are critical in turning high-risk ventures into successful enterprises. By continuously iterating on their designs, learning from failures, and leveraging strategic partnerships, SpaceX was able to overcome early challenges and achieve remarkable success.

This case study highlights the importance of:

- **Relentless Innovation**: Continuously improving and iterating on products and processes can lead to breakthrough innovations and long-term success.

- **Strategic Planning**: Developing a clear strategic plan and securing key partnerships can provide the resources and support needed to navigate challenges.
- **Persistence in the Face of Failure**: Embracing failures as learning opportunities and maintaining a commitment to the vision can drive a company to overcome obstacles and achieve its goals.

By applying these principles, businesses can navigate high-risk ventures and achieve transformative success, even in the face of significant challenges.

## Practical Tips for Making Informed Decisions

Here are some actionable tips to help you make informed decisions and take calculated risks:

### Do Your Homework

Conducting thorough research and gathering relevant information before making a decision is crucial for ensuring success. Understanding the market, industry trends, and potential challenges allows you to make informed choices and mitigate risks. Here are some steps and tips to help you do your homework effectively:

#### Steps to Conduct Thorough Research

1. **Identify Key Information Needs**: Determine what information is critical to your decision-making process. This could include market size, customer preferences, competitive landscape, regulatory environment, and technological advancements.

2. **Use Multiple Sources**: Rely on a variety of information sources to gain a comprehensive understanding. These sources can include industry reports, academic journals, news articles, government publications, and expert opinions. Diversifying your sources helps validate the information and provides different perspectives.
3. **Analyze Market Trends**: Look for trends and patterns in the market that could impact your decision. This involves understanding the historical context, current market conditions, and future projections. Pay attention to emerging technologies, consumer behavior changes, and economic indicators.
4. **Study the Competition**: Analyze your competitors to understand their strengths, weaknesses, strategies, and market positions. This can help you identify gaps in the market and potential opportunities for differentiation.
5. **Evaluate Potential Challenges**: Identify potential risks and challenges that could affect your decision. This includes considering factors such as market saturation, regulatory changes, supply chain disruptions, and economic downturns. Understanding these challenges allows you to develop strategies to address them.
6. **Seek Expert Advice**: Consult with industry experts, mentors, and professionals who have experience in the field. Their insights can provide valuable guidance and help you avoid common pitfalls.
7. **Conduct Primary Research**: When necessary, gather firsthand information through surveys, interviews, focus groups, and observations. Primary

research can provide specific insights tailored to your needs and validate secondary data.
8. **Synthesize and Interpret Data**: Organize the information you've gathered and analyze it to draw meaningful conclusions. Look for connections and insights that can inform your decision-making process.

**Tip: Use Multiple Sources to Validate Your Information**

To ensure you have a comprehensive understanding, it's important to validate your information using multiple sources. Here's how to do it:

- **Cross-Reference Data**: Compare information from different sources to check for consistency. If multiple sources report similar findings, it increases the reliability of the data.
- **Evaluate Source Credibility**: Assess the credibility of each source by considering its reputation, expertise, and potential biases. Academic journals, government publications, and industry reports are generally reliable, while news articles and blogs may require more scrutiny.
- **Stay Updated**: Markets and industries evolve rapidly, so ensure that your information is current. Regularly update your research to reflect the latest trends and developments.
- **Diversify Perspectives**: Seek information from a variety of perspectives, including those that challenge your assumptions. This helps you gain a balanced view and avoid confirmation bias.

**Example**

**Scenario**: You are considering launching a new health and wellness product in a competitive market.

1. **Identify Key Information Needs**:
   - Market demand for health and wellness products
   - Consumer preferences and behaviors
   - Regulatory requirements for health products
   - Competitor analysis
2. **Use Multiple Sources**:
   - Market reports from research firms like Nielsen and IBISWorld
   - Consumer surveys and focus groups
   - Articles from health industry publications
   - Regulatory guidelines from government health agencies
   - Competitor websites and annual reports
3. **Analyze Market Trends**:
   - Look for growth trends in the health and wellness sector
   - Identify popular health and wellness products and emerging trends (e.g., organic ingredients, personalized nutrition)
   - Monitor economic indicators that affect consumer spending on health products
4. **Study the Competition**:
   - Identify top competitors and analyze their product offerings, pricing, marketing strategies, and market share
   - Look for gaps in the market that your product could fill
5. **Evaluate Potential Challenges**:
   - Assess potential regulatory hurdles and compliance costs

- Consider supply chain risks for sourcing ingredients
- Evaluate market saturation and potential barriers to entry
6. **Seek Expert Advice**:
    - Consult with health industry experts, nutritionists, and regulatory consultants
7. **Conduct Primary Research**:
    - Conduct surveys to understand consumer preferences and willingness to pay for health products
    - Hold focus groups to gather feedback on product concepts
8. **Synthesize and Interpret Data**:
    - Analyze survey results and focus group feedback to refine your product concept
    - Compare secondary data from market reports with primary research findings

By thoroughly doing your homework, you can make well-informed decisions that are based on a comprehensive understanding of the market, industry trends, and potential challenges. This approach minimizes risks and increases the likelihood of success for your new venture.

## Seek Advice

Consulting with experts, mentors, and peers who have experience in the area you're exploring is an invaluable step in making informed decisions. Their insights can provide valuable perspectives, highlight potential opportunities, and help you avoid common pitfalls. Here's how to effectively seek advice and leverage the expertise of others:

**Steps to Seek Advice**

1. **Identify Relevant Experts and Mentors**: Look for individuals who have significant experience and success in the field related to your decision or project. These could include industry leaders, seasoned professionals, academics, or entrepreneurs who have navigated similar challenges.
2. **Join Professional Networks**: Become a member of professional organizations and networks related to your industry. These groups often provide access to a wealth of knowledge and connections that can support your decision-making process.
3. **Attend Industry Conferences and Events**: Participate in industry conferences, workshops, seminars, and webinars. These events offer opportunities to learn from experts, stay updated on industry trends, and network with peers.
4. **Engage in Online Communities**: Join online forums, discussion groups, and social media communities focused on your area of interest. Engaging in these platforms allows you to ask questions, share experiences, and receive feedback from a broader audience.
5. **Schedule One-on-One Meetings**: Reach out to experts and mentors for one-on-one meetings. Prepare specific questions and topics you want to discuss to make the most of their time and insights.
6. **Build Long-Term Relationships**: Cultivate relationships with mentors and peers over time. Regularly check in with them, share your progress, and seek their advice on new challenges. Building

a strong network of trusted advisors can provide ongoing support and guidance.

### Tip: Join Professional Networks and Attend Industry Conferences

Joining professional networks and attending industry conferences are effective ways to connect with knowledgeable individuals and stay informed about the latest developments in your field. Here's how to maximize these opportunities:

- **Professional Networks**:
    - **Membership Benefits**: Many professional organizations offer exclusive resources, such as industry reports, webinars, and training sessions. Take advantage of these benefits to enhance your knowledge and skills.
    - **Networking Opportunities**: Participate in networking events, such as meetups, mixers, and online networking sessions. Use these occasions to introduce yourself, share your interests, and build connections with like-minded professionals.
    - **Mentorship Programs**: Some organizations offer formal mentorship programs that pair you with experienced mentors. Enroll in these programs to receive personalized guidance and support.
- **Industry Conferences**:
    - **Plan Ahead**: Research upcoming conferences and select those that align with your interests and goals. Register early and

plan your schedule to attend key sessions, workshops, and networking events.
- **Engage with Speakers and Attendees**: Take advantage of Q&A sessions, panel discussions, and networking breaks to engage with speakers and fellow attendees. Prepare thoughtful questions and be ready to discuss your own experiences and challenges.
- **Follow Up**: After the conference, follow up with new contacts by sending personalized emails or connecting on professional networking sites like LinkedIn. Maintain these connections by staying in touch and offering support or collaboration opportunities.

### Example

**Scenario**: You are planning to launch a tech startup focused on developing innovative software solutions for small businesses. Seeking advice from experts and mentors can provide you with valuable insights and help you navigate the challenges of launching a new venture.

1. **Identify Relevant Experts and Mentors**:
     - Experienced tech entrepreneurs who have successfully launched and scaled startups
     - Industry analysts who understand market trends and competitive dynamics
     - Investors who specialize in tech startups and can provide funding and strategic advice
2. **Join Professional Networks**:

- Become a member of organizations like the Tech Entrepreneurs Network or the Small Business Software Association
- Participate in local startup incubators or accelerators that offer mentorship and resources

3. **Attend Industry Conferences and Events**:
   - Attend conferences such as TechCrunch Disrupt, Startup Grind, and SaaStr Annual
   - Participate in regional tech meetups and startup pitch events
4. **Engage in Online Communities**:
   - Join LinkedIn groups focused on tech entrepreneurship and small business software
   - Participate in Reddit forums like r/startups and r/entrepreneur
5. **Schedule One-on-One Meetings**:
   - Reach out to potential mentors and experts for coffee meetings or video calls
   - Prepare questions about funding strategies, market entry, product development, and scaling operations
6. **Build Long-Term Relationships**:
   - Regularly update your mentors on your progress and seek their advice on new challenges
   - Attend networking events and continue to build your professional network

By seeking advice from experienced professionals and engaging with industry networks, you can gain valuable insights, avoid common pitfalls, and increase your chances of success. This approach ensures that you are well-informed and supported as you navigate the complexities of launching and growing your tech startup.

## Start Small

If possible, test your idea on a smaller scale before committing significant resources. This approach allows you to learn and make adjustments without exposing yourself to excessive risk. Starting small helps you validate your concept, gather feedback, and refine your strategy, ultimately increasing the likelihood of success.

### Steps to Start Small

1. **Develop a Pilot Program**: Implement a pilot program to test your idea in a controlled and limited setting. This allows you to gather data, assess feasibility, and identify any issues that need to be addressed before a full-scale launch.
2. **Create Prototypes**: Develop prototypes of your product to test functionality, design, and user experience. Prototypes can help you identify flaws and areas for improvement, as well as demonstrate your concept to potential investors and customers.
3. **Conduct Market Trials**: Launch a market trial to introduce your product or service to a small segment of your target market. This helps you gauge customer interest, test marketing strategies, and collect valuable feedback.
4. **Monitor and Evaluate**: Continuously monitor the performance of your pilot program, prototype, or market trial. Evaluate the results to determine what works well and what needs to be adjusted. Use this information to make informed decisions about scaling up.

5. **Iterate and Improve**: Based on the feedback and data collected, iterate on your product or service. Make necessary improvements and refinements to enhance its effectiveness and appeal.

**Tip: Consider Pilot Programs, Prototypes, or Market Trials as Initial Steps**

By starting small with pilot programs, prototypes, or market trials, you can minimize risks and increase your chances of success. Here's how to effectively implement these initial steps:

- **Pilot Programs**:
    - **Define Objectives**: Clearly outline the goals of your pilot program. What specific aspects of your idea do you want to test? Define success criteria and key performance indicators (KPIs).
    - **Select a Test Group**: Choose a representative sample of your target audience to participate in the pilot program. Ensure that this group provides diverse feedback and insights.
    - **Collect Data**: Use surveys, interviews, and analytics to gather data on participant experiences and outcomes. Analyze this data to assess the feasibility and effectiveness of your idea.
- **Prototypes**:
    - **Design Iterations**: Start with basic prototypes and gradually refine them based on feedback. Create multiple iterations to test different aspects of your product.

- User Testing: Involve potential users in the testing process. Observe how they interact with the prototype and gather feedback on usability, design, and functionality.
- Demonstrate Value: Use prototypes to showcase your concept to stakeholders, including investors, partners, and customers. Highlight the benefits and potential impact of your product.
- **Market Trials**:
    - Segment the Market: Identify a specific segment of your target market for the trial. This could be a geographic area, demographic group, or customer type.
    - Launch Strategically: Implement a soft launch with limited marketing efforts to introduce your product or service. Monitor customer reactions and adjust your strategy accordingly.
    - Gather Feedback: Collect feedback from trial participants through surveys, reviews, and direct interactions. Use this feedback to refine your product and marketing approach.

### Example

**Scenario**: You are developing a new mobile app designed to help users manage their personal finances. To minimize risk, you decide to start small by creating a prototype and conducting a market trial.

1. **Develop a Pilot Program**:

- Define objectives: Test the app's core features, user interface, and overall user experience.
- Select a test group: Recruit a small group of users from diverse backgrounds to participate in the pilot program.

2. **Create Prototypes**:
   - Design iterations: Develop several versions of the app's interface and functionality. Start with a basic prototype and refine it based on user feedback.
   - User testing: Conduct user testing sessions where participants interact with the app and provide feedback on usability and design.

3. **Conduct Market Trials**:
   - Segment the market: Choose a specific demographic group, such as young professionals, for the market trial.
   - Launch strategically: Introduce the app to this group through targeted marketing efforts, such as social media ads and influencer partnerships.
   - Gather feedback: Collect feedback through in-app surveys, user reviews, and direct interactions with trial participants.

4. **Monitor and Evaluate**:
   - Monitor performance: Track key metrics, such as user engagement, retention rates, and feedback scores.
   - Evaluate results: Analyze the data to determine the app's strengths and areas for improvement.

5. **Iterate and Improve**:

- Based on the feedback and data collected, make necessary improvements to the app's features, design, and user experience.
- Prepare for a larger-scale launch by addressing any identified issues and refining your marketing strategy.

By starting small and testing your idea on a limited scale, you can gather valuable insights, reduce risks, and increase the likelihood of success when you eventually scale up. This approach ensures that you make informed decisions and continuously improve your product or service based on real-world feedback.

## Develop a Contingency Plan

Preparing for potential setbacks by having a contingency plan in place is crucial for navigating unexpected challenges. A well-developed contingency plan identifies alternative strategies and resources that can help you adapt and respond effectively when things don't go as planned.

### Steps to Develop a Contingency Plan

1. **Identify Potential Risks and Setbacks**: Start by listing possible risks and setbacks that could impact your project or decision. These might include financial challenges, supply chain disruptions, regulatory changes, market shifts, or internal issues such as key personnel leaving.
2. **Assess Impact and Likelihood**: Evaluate the potential impact and likelihood of each identified risk. This helps prioritize which risks need detailed

contingency plans and which can be monitored with less urgency.
3. **Develop Alternative Strategies**: For each high-impact risk, brainstorm alternative strategies that could mitigate the adverse effects. Consider different scenarios and how you might respond to each one. These strategies should be specific, actionable, and realistic.
4. **Allocate Resources**: Identify the resources needed to implement your contingency plans. This could include financial reserves, additional personnel, equipment, or external partnerships. Ensure that these resources are accessible when needed.
5. **Assign Responsibilities**: Clearly define who will be responsible for implementing each part of the contingency plan. Assign roles and ensure that everyone involved understands their responsibilities and the plan's objectives.
6. **Create a Communication Plan**: Develop a communication plan to keep stakeholders informed during a crisis. This should include key contacts, communication channels, and protocols for updating team members, customers, and partners.
7. **Test and Train**: Conduct drills or simulations to test your contingency plans. This helps identify any weaknesses and ensures that your team is prepared to act quickly and effectively. Provide training to ensure that everyone knows how to execute the plan.
8. **Monitor and Review**: Continuously monitor the environment for changes that could impact your risks. Regularly review and update your

contingency plans as new information becomes available or as circumstances change.

### Tip: Regularly Review and Update Your Contingency Plans

To ensure your contingency plans remain effective, it's essential to regularly review and update them. Here's how to keep your plans current:

- **Schedule Regular Reviews**: Set regular intervals (e.g., quarterly or biannually) to review your contingency plans. Assess whether the identified risks are still relevant and if new risks have emerged.
- **Incorporate Feedback**: After conducting drills or responding to actual incidents, gather feedback from your team and stakeholders. Use this feedback to refine and improve your plans.
- **Stay Informed**: Keep up-to-date with industry trends, regulatory changes, and other external factors that could affect your risks. Adjust your contingency plans accordingly.
- **Document Changes**: Maintain a detailed record of all changes made to your contingency plans. Ensure that updated plans are easily accessible to all relevant parties.

### Example

**Scenario**: You are running a manufacturing company that relies on a global supply chain. Developing a contingency plan can help you prepare for potential disruptions.

1. **Identify Potential Risks and Setbacks**:

- Supply chain disruptions (e.g., due to natural disasters, geopolitical issues, or pandemics)
- Equipment failures
- Financial challenges (e.g., cash flow issues)
- Regulatory changes

2. **Assess Impact and Likelihood**:
   - High impact, high likelihood: Supply chain disruptions
   - High impact, medium likelihood: Equipment failures
   - Medium impact, medium likelihood: Financial challenges
   - Medium impact, low likelihood: Regulatory changes

3. **Develop Alternative Strategies**:
   - **Supply Chain Disruptions**:
     - Diversify suppliers to reduce dependency on a single source
     - Establish agreements with backup suppliers
     - Increase inventory of critical components
   - **Equipment Failures**:
     - Implement a preventive maintenance program
     - Keep spare parts and backup equipment on hand
     - Train staff on quick repair and troubleshooting techniques
   - **Financial Challenges**:
     - Maintain a financial reserve or line of credit

- Implement cost-cutting measures if needed
- Review and optimize cash flow management
   - **Regulatory Changes**:
     - Stay informed about potential regulatory changes
     - Engage with industry associations and lobby for favorable policies
     - Develop compliance plans for different regulatory scenarios

4. **Allocate Resources**:
   - Financial reserves for emergencies
   - Backup suppliers and increased inventory
   - Spare parts and maintenance tools
   - Staff training programs
5. **Assign Responsibilities**:
   - Supply chain manager to oversee supplier diversification and backup agreements
   - Maintenance team to implement and manage preventive maintenance
   - Financial officer to manage financial reserves and cash flow
   - Compliance officer to monitor regulatory changes and update plans
6. **Create a Communication Plan**:
   - Key contacts: Supply chain manager, maintenance team leader, financial officer, compliance officer
   - Communication channels: Email, phone, internal messaging system
   - Protocols: Regular updates, emergency notifications, stakeholder briefings
7. **Test and Train**:

- Conduct supply chain disruption simulations
- Perform equipment failure drills
- Financial stress tests
- Regulatory compliance exercises

8. **Monitor and Review**:
   - Schedule quarterly reviews of contingency plans
   - Incorporate feedback from drills and real incidents
   - Stay updated on industry and regulatory developments

By developing a comprehensive contingency plan, you can prepare for potential setbacks and navigate unexpected challenges more effectively. Regularly reviewing and updating your plans ensures that you remain agile and responsive to changing circumstances, ultimately safeguarding your business and its operations.

## Trust Your Instincts

While data and analysis are crucial for making informed decisions, it's important not to ignore your intuition. Your instincts, shaped by your experiences and insights, can often guide you in the right direction. Trusting your instincts can complement the logical decision-making process, providing a holistic approach to evaluating opportunities and risks.

### Steps to Trust Your Instincts

1. **Acknowledge the Role of Intuition**: Recognize that intuition is a valuable component of decision-making. It often arises from subconscious processing of past experiences, knowledge, and

patterns that your conscious mind may not immediately recognize.
2. **Combine Intuition with Data**: Use intuition alongside data and analysis. While data provides objective insights, intuition can offer subjective understanding that complements the facts. This balanced approach can lead to more well-rounded decisions.
3. **Reflect on Past Experiences**: Take time to reflect on past situations where your intuition played a key role in successful outcomes. Understanding how your instincts guided you in the past can reinforce your confidence in using them for future decisions.
4. **Cultivate Self-Awareness**: Develop self-awareness by regularly reflecting on your thoughts, feelings, and reactions. This practice helps you distinguish between genuine intuition and emotional responses such as fear or wishful thinking.
5. **Practice Mindfulness**: Engage in mindfulness practices such as meditation or deep breathing to enhance your ability to tune into your instincts. Mindfulness can help you clear mental clutter and focus on your inner voice.
6. **Test Your Intuition**: When possible, test your intuitive insights with small-scale experiments or pilot projects. This allows you to validate your instincts without committing significant resources upfront.
7. **Seek Diverse Perspectives**: Discuss your intuitions with trusted advisors, mentors, or peers. Their feedback can provide additional perspectives and help you evaluate the validity of your instincts.

### Tip: Reflect on Past Experiences Where Your Intuition Played a Role in Successful Outcomes

Reflecting on past experiences can help you understand the value of intuition and build confidence in trusting it. Here's how to do it effectively:

- **Identify Key Decisions**: List significant decisions you've made in your personal or professional life where intuition played a role. Focus on those that led to positive outcomes.
- **Analyze the Process**: Reflect on how you arrived at those decisions. What specific instincts or gut feelings did you have? How did they influence your actions?
- **Evaluate Outcomes**: Assess the results of those decisions. How did your intuition contribute to the success? What did you learn from these experiences?
- **Document Insights**: Keep a journal of these reflections to track patterns and deepen your understanding of how intuition works for you. This record can serve as a valuable resource for future decision-making.

### Example

**Scenario**: You are an entrepreneur considering a new business venture. While market research and data analysis support the idea, your intuition is signaling potential challenges that the data does not fully capture.

1. **Acknowledge the Role of Intuition**:
   - Recognize that your gut feeling might be picking up on subtle cues or past

experiences that are not immediately evident in the data.

2. **Combine Intuition with Data**:
   - Use the data to inform your decision while also considering your intuitive insights. Ask yourself what your instincts are telling you and why.
3. **Reflect on Past Experiences**:
   - Recall a previous business venture where your intuition played a critical role. For example, you might remember a time when you trusted your gut feeling about a potential partner and it led to a successful collaboration.
4. **Cultivate Self-Awareness**:
   - Regularly engage in self-reflection to understand your thought processes and emotional responses. This practice helps you differentiate between true intuition and emotional bias.
5. **Practice Mindfulness**:
   - Incorporate mindfulness techniques into your routine to enhance clarity and focus. This can help you tune into your instincts more effectively.
6. **Test Your Intuition**:
   - Consider launching a pilot project or small-scale trial to test the viability of the new venture. This allows you to validate your intuition with minimal risk.
7. **Seek Diverse Perspectives**:
   - Discuss your intuitive insights with mentors or industry experts. Their feedback can help

you evaluate the potential challenges and opportunities your instincts are highlighting.

By trusting your instincts and integrating them with data and analysis, you can make more comprehensive and informed decisions. Reflecting on past successes where intuition played a key role reinforces the value of trusting your gut feelings, providing a balanced approach to navigating new opportunities and risks.

## Evaluate Regularly

Continuously assessing the progress and outcomes of your decisions is crucial for long-term success. Regular evaluation allows you to identify what's working, what's not, and what needs adjustment. By being willing to adapt and make changes based on new information and evolving circumstances, you can ensure that your strategies remain effective and aligned with your goals.

### Steps to Evaluate Regularly

1. **Set Clear Metrics and Goals**: Define specific, measurable metrics and goals for your decision or project. These benchmarks will help you gauge progress and determine the effectiveness of your actions.
2. **Gather Data and Feedback**: Collect data on your performance against the set metrics. This can include quantitative data such as sales figures, customer feedback, or productivity stats, as well as qualitative insights from team members and stakeholders.
3. **Analyze Performance**: Regularly analyze the collected data to identify trends, successes, and

areas for improvement. Look for patterns that indicate whether your strategies are achieving the desired outcomes.
4. **Identify Challenges and Opportunities**: Use the analysis to pinpoint challenges that need addressing and opportunities that can be leveraged. This step is crucial for proactive management and continuous improvement.
5. **Make Informed Adjustments**: Based on your analysis, make necessary adjustments to your strategies and plans. This could involve reallocating resources, changing tactics, or setting new priorities.
6. **Document Changes and Learnings**: Keep a detailed record of the changes made and the reasons behind them. Documenting your learnings helps you build a knowledge base for future decision-making and ensures continuity if team members change.
7. **Communicate with Stakeholders**: Regularly update relevant stakeholders on progress and changes. Transparent communication fosters trust and ensures everyone is aligned with the current direction.
8. **Schedule Regular Review Sessions**: Establish a routine for reviewing progress and making adjustments. Regular review sessions help maintain focus and accountability, allowing you to respond swiftly to new information and changing circumstances.

**Tip: Schedule Regular Review Sessions to Monitor Progress and Make Necessary Adjustments**

Scheduling regular review sessions is key to maintaining momentum and ensuring continuous improvement. Here's how to implement this practice effectively:

- **Set a Review Schedule**: Determine the frequency of your review sessions based on the nature and timeline of your project. Common intervals include weekly, monthly, or quarterly reviews.
- **Prepare for Each Session**: Before each review session, gather the latest data, feedback, and any relevant updates. Prepare an agenda that outlines the key points to be discussed.
- **Involve Key Stakeholders**: Ensure that all relevant team members and stakeholders are involved in the review sessions. Their input is valuable for a comprehensive evaluation.
- **Focus on Actionable Insights**: During the review, focus on identifying actionable insights rather than just reporting on data. Discuss what the data means and how it should inform your next steps.
- **Track Follow-Up Actions**: Assign responsibilities for any follow-up actions decided during the review session. Keep track of these actions and their outcomes in subsequent sessions to ensure accountability.

### Example

**Scenario**: You are leading a project to develop a new software application. Regular evaluation is crucial to ensure the project stays on track and meets its goals.

1. **Set Clear Metrics and Goals**:

- Metrics: Project milestones, completion dates, budget adherence, user satisfaction scores
- Goals: Deliver a functional prototype by the end of Q1, complete user testing by Q2, launch the final product by Q3

2. **Gather Data and Feedback**:
   - Collect data on milestone completion, budget status, and user feedback from testing phases
   - Obtain feedback from the development team on progress and any challenges faced
3. **Analyze Performance**:
   - Review the collected data to determine if the project is on schedule and within budget
   - Analyze user feedback to identify any common issues or areas for improvement
4. **Identify Challenges and Opportunities**:
   - Challenge: Delays in the development phase due to unforeseen technical issues
   - Opportunity: Positive user feedback on the prototype's usability, indicating a strong market fit
5. **Make Informed Adjustments**:
   - Adjust the project timeline to accommodate additional development time for resolving technical issues
   - Reallocate budget to invest in additional testing resources to further refine the user experience
6. **Document Changes and Learnings**:
   - Document the adjusted timeline and budget changes

- Record insights from user feedback and team discussions to inform future development cycles
7. **Communicate with Stakeholders**:
    - Provide regular updates to stakeholders, including progress reports and explanations for any changes
    - Hold meetings with the development team to ensure alignment and address any concerns
8. **Schedule Regular Review Sessions**:
    - Schedule monthly review sessions to monitor progress and make necessary adjustments
    - Use these sessions to track follow-up actions and ensure accountability for assigned tasks

By regularly evaluating progress and being willing to adapt based on new information, you can keep your project on track and increase the likelihood of success. This approach ensures that you are responsive to challenges and opportunities, continuously improving your strategies and achieving your goals.

In conclusion, taking calculated risks involves a strategic and thoughtful approach to decision-making. By understanding the difference between reckless and calculated risks, using assessment tools, learning from successful examples, and applying practical tips, you can make informed choices that lead to growth and success. Embrace the mindset of calculated risk-taking and unlock new opportunities for achieving your goals.

# Chapter 4

# Overcoming Obstacles

## Common Challenges Faced When Taking Risks

Taking risks is inherently challenging and can be fraught with obstacles. Some of the most common challenges include:

1. **Fear of Failure**: The anxiety of not achieving desired outcomes can prevent many from taking risks. This fear often stems from concerns about personal reputation, financial loss, or wasted time and effort.
2. **Resource Limitations**: Limited financial, human, or material resources can constrain the ability to take bold actions and explore new opportunities.
3. **Lack of Support**: Not having the backing of family, friends, colleagues, or mentors can make taking risks feel isolating and overwhelming.
4. **Uncertainty and Ambiguity**: The unknown aspects of taking risks can cause significant stress and hesitation. This includes uncertainty about market conditions, customer reactions, or technical feasibility.
5. **Internal Doubts**: Self-doubt and lack of confidence can undermine the willingness to take risks and pursue ambitious goals.

## Strategies for Resilience and Perseverance

Resilience and perseverance are crucial for overcoming obstacles when taking risks. Here are some effective strategies to build and maintain these qualities:

1. **Develop a Growth Mindset**: Embrace the belief that abilities and intelligence can be developed through effort and learning. This mindset encourages resilience in the face of setbacks and a willingness to learn from mistakes.
    - **Example**: View challenges as opportunities for growth rather than threats to success.
2. **Set Realistic and Incremental Goals**: Break down larger goals into smaller, manageable tasks. Achieving these incremental milestones builds momentum and reinforces perseverance.
    - **Example**: If launching a new product, start with developing a prototype before moving to full-scale production.
3. **Build a Strong Support Network**: Surround yourself with supportive people who encourage and believe in you. Mentors, peers, and loved ones can provide valuable guidance and reassurance.
    - **Example**: Join professional networks or support groups relevant to your field.
4. **Practice Self-Care**: Maintain physical and mental well-being to enhance your capacity for resilience. Regular exercise, healthy eating, adequate sleep, and mindfulness practices can help manage stress and keep you focused.
    - **Example**: Incorporate daily meditation or yoga into your routine to stay grounded and calm.
5. **Embrace Flexibility and Adaptability**: Be willing to adjust your plans and strategies based on new

information and changing circumstances. Flexibility helps you stay resilient when things don't go as expected.
    - **Example**: If a business strategy isn't working, pivot to a new approach based on market feedback.

## Stories of Overcoming Setbacks

Real-life stories of individuals who have faced and overcome significant obstacles can provide inspiration and practical insights. Here are a few examples:

1. **J.K. Rowling**: Before becoming one of the most successful authors in the world, J.K. Rowling faced numerous rejections from publishers. Her persistence and determination to share her story eventually led to the creation of the beloved Harry Potter series, inspiring millions worldwide.
    - **Lesson**: Persistence in the face of repeated failure can lead to extraordinary success.
2. **Elon Musk**: Known for his ambitious ventures, Elon Musk has faced multiple failures and setbacks in his career. From the early struggles of SpaceX to the near-collapse of Tesla, Musk's ability to confront and overcome fear has driven him to achieve groundbreaking successes in technology and space exploration.
    - **Lesson**: Innovation and resilience can turn high-risk ventures into successful enterprises.
3. **Oprah Winfrey**: Overcoming a challenging childhood marked by poverty and abuse, Oprah Winfrey faced significant obstacles in her path to

success. Her resilience and refusal to be defined by her past enabled her to become a media mogul and influential figure, inspiring countless individuals.
- **Lesson**: Resilience and self-belief can help overcome even the most difficult circumstances.

## Techniques for Maintaining Motivation and Focus

Maintaining motivation and focus is essential for persevering through obstacles. Here are some techniques to help you stay driven and concentrated:

1. **Set Clear and Achievable Goals**: Having specific, measurable goals gives you a clear direction and a sense of purpose.
    - **Example**: Use SMART goals (Specific, Measurable, Achievable, Relevant, Time-bound) to create a structured plan.
2. **Visualize Success**: Regularly visualize the successful achievement of your goals. This can boost motivation and reinforce your commitment to your objectives.
    - **Example**: Spend a few minutes each day imagining the positive outcomes of your efforts.
3. **Celebrate Small Wins**: Recognize and celebrate small milestones along the way. This keeps morale high and maintains momentum.
    - **Example**: Reward yourself after completing significant tasks or reaching important milestones.

4. **Stay Organized and Prioritize**: Use tools like to-do lists, calendars, and project management software to stay organized and prioritize tasks effectively.
    - **Example**: Break your tasks into daily to-do lists to ensure consistent progress.
5. **Maintain a Positive Attitude**: Focus on positive thinking and self-affirmation to build confidence and reduce stress.
    - **Example**: Practice gratitude by noting down things you are thankful for each day.
6. **Seek Inspiration**: Surround yourself with motivational content such as books, podcasts, and videos. Learning from others who have overcome obstacles can keep you inspired and motivated.
    - **Example**: Listen to motivational podcasts during your commute or exercise routine.

By understanding common challenges, employing strategies for resilience and perseverance, learning from inspirational stories, and utilizing techniques to maintain motivation and focus, you can overcome obstacles and achieve your goals despite the risks involved.

# Chapter 5

# The Mindset of a Risk Taker

## Developing a Growth Mindset

A growth mindset is the belief that abilities and intelligence can be developed through dedication, hard work, and continuous learning. This mindset is essential for risk-takers, as it encourages resilience, curiosity, and a willingness to embrace challenges.

### Steps to Develop a Growth Mindset

#### Embrace Challenges

Viewing challenges as opportunities to learn and grow rather than as obstacles is a crucial component of developing a growth mindset. Accepting that difficulties are part of the process helps you stay motivated and persistent, enabling you to overcome obstacles and achieve your goals.

##### Steps to Embrace Challenges

1. **Shift Your Perspective**: Reframe your mindset to see challenges as valuable learning experiences. Instead of viewing difficulties as setbacks, recognize them as chances to develop new skills and gain knowledge.
    - **Example**: When faced with a difficult project, focus on the skills you will develop and the knowledge you will gain rather than the possibility of failure.

2. **Set Learning Goals**: In addition to performance goals, set specific learning goals for yourself. This shifts your focus from merely achieving an outcome to also valuing the learning process.
    - **Example**: Instead of only aiming to complete a project successfully, set a goal to learn a new project management tool or improve your problem-solving abilities.
3. **Practice Self-Compassion**: Be kind to yourself when facing challenges. Understand that encountering difficulties is a normal part of growth, and avoid harsh self-criticism.
    - **Example**: If you make a mistake, acknowledge it without negative self-talk and remind yourself that it's an opportunity to learn and improve.
4. **Break Down Challenges**: Divide large, daunting challenges into smaller, manageable tasks. This makes them less overwhelming and allows you to make steady progress.
    - **Example**: If you're tasked with launching a new product, break the project down into phases such as market research, product development, and marketing strategy.
5. **Celebrate Progress**: Recognize and celebrate your progress, no matter how small. Celebrating achievements, even minor ones, can boost your motivation and reinforce a positive attitude towards challenges.
    - **Example**: After completing a challenging task, reward yourself with a small treat or take a moment to reflect on your accomplishment.

6. **Seek Support and Feedback**: Don't hesitate to seek help from others when facing challenges. Collaborating with peers or mentors can provide new perspectives and solutions.
    - **Example**: If you're struggling with a complex problem, discuss it with a colleague or mentor who might offer valuable insights and suggestions.

**Example**

**Scenario**: You are assigned to lead a difficult project that involves integrating a new software system across multiple departments in your organization.

1. **Shift Your Perspective**:
    - Instead of worrying about the possibility of failure, focus on the opportunity to enhance your project management skills and deepen your understanding of the software.
2. **Set Learning Goals**:
    - Set a goal to become proficient in the new software and to learn best practices for cross-departmental collaboration.
3. **Practice Self-Compassion**:
    - When you encounter setbacks, remind yourself that it's normal to face challenges with complex projects. Treat yourself with the same kindness and encouragement you would offer to a friend.
4. **Break Down Challenges**:
    - Divide the project into smaller tasks such as initial planning, stakeholder meetings, software training sessions, pilot testing, and

full implementation. Tackle each phase systematically.
5. **Celebrate Progress**:
     - Celebrate milestones such as completing the software training phase or successfully conducting pilot testing. Acknowledge your hard work and progress with your team.
6. **Seek Support and Feedback**:
     - Regularly consult with team members and IT specialists to address any issues that arise. Solicit feedback from users during the pilot testing phase to identify areas for improvement.

By embracing challenges with a positive and proactive mindset, you can transform obstacles into opportunities for growth and development. This approach helps you stay motivated, persistent, and resilient in the face of difficulties, ultimately leading to greater success and fulfillment.

## Learn from Criticism

Constructive criticism provides valuable feedback that can help you improve. Instead of feeling defensive, use feedback to enhance your skills and performance. Embracing criticism as a tool for growth allows you to continuously develop and achieve higher levels of success.

### Steps to Learn from Criticism

1. **Receive Feedback Openly**: Approach feedback with an open mind and a willingness to learn. Understand that criticism is not a personal attack but an opportunity for improvement.

- **Example**: When someone offers feedback, listen attentively without interrupting or immediately defending yourself.
2. **Analyze the Feedback**: Carefully consider the points raised in the feedback. Identify specific areas where you can improve and think about how the feedback relates to your goals and performance.
    - **Example**: If you receive critical feedback on a presentation, analyze the specific aspects mentioned, such as content clarity, delivery style, or visual aids.
3. **Ask Clarifying Questions**: If any part of the feedback is unclear, don't hesitate to ask for clarification. Understanding the feedback fully ensures that you can effectively address the areas for improvement.
    - **Example**: Ask questions like, "Can you give me an example of where I lost the audience's attention?" or "What specific changes would you suggest for my slides?"
4. **Reflect and Plan**: Reflect on the feedback and develop a plan for how you will implement the suggested improvements. Set specific, actionable goals to address the feedback.
    - **Example**: Create a plan to improve your presentation skills, such as practicing public speaking, simplifying your slides, or using more engaging visuals.
5. **Practice and Implement Changes**: Put your plan into action by practicing the areas you need to improve. Continuous practice helps reinforce new skills and makes them a natural part of your performance.

- **Example**: Practice your next presentation multiple times, focusing on the areas where you received critical feedback. Seek additional opportunities to present and apply the feedback.
6. **Seek Continuous Feedback**: Feedback is an ongoing process. Regularly seek feedback from others to continue improving and refining your skills.
    - **Example**: After implementing changes, ask for feedback on your next presentation to see if the improvements were effective and identify any new areas for growth.

## Example

**Scenario**: You receive critical feedback on a presentation you delivered to your team. The feedback includes comments on your delivery style being too fast, the slides being cluttered, and the content lacking clear structure.

1. **Receive Feedback Openly**:
    - Listen to the feedback without interrupting. Thank your colleagues for their input and express your willingness to improve.
2. **Analyze the Feedback**:
    - Review the specific points mentioned: speaking too fast, cluttered slides, and lack of clear structure. Understand how these aspects affected the overall effectiveness of your presentation.
3. **Ask Clarifying Questions**:
    - Ask your colleagues for specific examples of when you spoke too fast and which slides appeared cluttered. Inquire about

suggestions for structuring your content more clearly.
   4. **Reflect and Plan**:
      - Reflect on the feedback and develop a plan to address each point. Set goals such as speaking at a measured pace, simplifying slide design, and organizing content with a clear introduction, body, and conclusion.
   5. **Practice and Implement Changes**:
      - Practice your presentation skills by recording yourself and adjusting your speaking pace. Redesign your slides to include only essential information and use a clean, consistent layout. Rehearse your presentation with a clear structure.
   6. **Seek Continuous Feedback**:
      - Deliver your next presentation and ask for feedback on the improvements. Seek input on whether the changes made a positive difference and if there are any new areas for improvement.

By learning from criticism and using it to enhance your skills and performance, you can continuously improve and achieve greater success. This approach fosters a growth mindset, encourages continuous learning, and helps you develop resilience in the face of challenges.

## Celebrate Effort

Recognizing and rewarding your efforts, not just your successes, is crucial for maintaining motivation and reinforcing the value of persistence and dedication. Celebrating effort helps build a positive mindset and encourages continued hard work, regardless of the immediate outcomes.

### Steps to Celebrate Effort

1. **Acknowledge Your Hard Work**: Regularly take time to acknowledge the effort you've put into your tasks and projects. Recognize the dedication and persistence required to tackle challenges and complete difficult tasks.
    - **Example**: After preparing extensively for a big meeting, take a moment to appreciate the hard work and preparation you put into it, regardless of how the meeting goes.
2. **Set Effort-Based Goals**: In addition to outcome-based goals, set goals that focus on the effort you will put into achieving them. This helps shift the focus from results to the process of working hard and staying dedicated.
    - **Example**: Instead of only setting a goal to close a deal, set a goal to make a certain number of quality client presentations.
3. **Reward Yourself**: Create a system of rewards for yourself that acknowledges your effort. These rewards can be small treats, breaks, or activities you enjoy, and they help reinforce the value of your hard work.
    - **Example**: After completing a challenging project, reward yourself with a favorite meal, a relaxing evening, or a fun activity.
4. **Share Your Efforts**: Share your hard work and dedication with others, whether it's colleagues, friends, or family. Positive reinforcement from others can boost your morale and motivate you to continue putting in the effort.

- **Example**: Discuss the preparation you did for a big presentation with a colleague or friend and share how proud you are of your hard work.
5. **Reflect on Your Progress**: Regularly reflect on the progress you've made through your efforts. Look back at where you started and how far you've come, acknowledging the hard work that got you there.
   - **Example**: Keep a journal where you document the efforts you've put into your projects and tasks, and periodically review it to see your growth.
6. **Encourage Others**: Celebrate the efforts of those around you, whether it's team members, peers, or employees. Recognizing their hard work fosters a supportive environment and encourages a culture of persistence and dedication.
   - **Example**: Compliment a colleague on the effort they put into a report or presentation, regardless of the outcome.

## Example

**Scenario**: You've been preparing for weeks for a big meeting with potential investors. The meeting itself is important, but so is the effort and dedication you've put into getting ready for it.

1. **Acknowledge Your Hard Work**:
   - Recognize the time and energy you invested in researching, creating materials, and practicing your presentation. Take a moment to appreciate your commitment and dedication.

2. **Set Effort-Based Goals**:
   - Set a goal to thoroughly prepare for the meeting by completing specific tasks, such as developing a detailed pitch deck, rehearsing your presentation multiple times, and gathering all necessary data.
3. **Reward Yourself**:
   - Plan a small reward for yourself after the meeting, such as treating yourself to your favorite coffee or taking a relaxing walk. This reward acknowledges your hard work, independent of the meeting's outcome.
4. **Share Your Efforts**:
   - Talk to a friend or family member about the preparation you did for the meeting. Share how much effort you put into it and express pride in your dedication.
5. **Reflect on Your Progress**:
   - Reflect on how much you've learned and grown through the preparation process. Consider how your skills have improved and how you've become more knowledgeable about your project or proposal.
6. **Encourage Others**:
   - If you're working with a team, acknowledge their hard work as well. Celebrate the collective effort and dedication that everyone contributed to preparing for the meeting.

By celebrating effort, you reinforce the importance of persistence and dedication, fostering a positive and resilient mindset. This approach helps you stay motivated and committed to your goals, regardless of immediate outcomes, and encourages continuous hard work and improvement.

## Persist Through Setbacks

Understanding that setbacks are a natural part of the learning process is crucial for long-term success. Instead of viewing setbacks as reasons to give up, use them as stepping stones to success. Embracing this mindset helps you stay resilient and motivated, turning challenges into opportunities for growth.

### Steps to Persist Through Setbacks

1. **Acknowledge the Setback**: Recognize and accept that setbacks are a normal part of any journey. Acknowledging them helps you face the situation head-on and prepares you to address the challenges.
    - **Example**: If a business venture fails, admit that the failure occurred and understand that it is a part of the entrepreneurial process.
2. **Analyze What Went Wrong**: Take the time to reflect on the setback and identify the factors that contributed to it. Analyzing what went wrong provides valuable insights and lessons that can inform future decisions.
    - **Example**: Conduct a thorough post-mortem analysis of the failed venture. Look into areas such as market research, product development, marketing strategies, and financial management.
3. **Learn from the Experience**: Extract lessons from the setback to improve your skills and strategies.

Treat each setback as a learning opportunity that can make you more capable and prepared for future challenges.
    - **Example**: Identify key takeaways from the failed venture, such as the importance of better market research or the need for a more flexible business model.
4. **Develop a Plan for Improvement**: Create a plan to address the issues identified during your analysis. Outline specific actions you will take to prevent similar setbacks in the future and to build on the lessons learned.
    - **Example**: Develop a new business plan that incorporates detailed market research, a more robust marketing strategy, and contingency plans for financial management.
5. **Stay Positive and Motivated**: Maintain a positive attitude and keep your long-term goals in mind. Focus on your progress and the knowledge you've gained rather than dwelling on the setback.
    - **Example**: Remind yourself of your initial motivation for starting the venture and how the experience has made you stronger and more knowledgeable.
6. **Take Action and Move Forward**: Implement the improvements and continue working towards your goals. Taking proactive steps helps you regain momentum and move past the setback.
    - **Example**: Launch a new venture or project with the insights and strategies you've developed from your previous experience.

**Example**

**Scenario**: You launch a business venture, but it fails to gain traction in the market and ultimately has to be shut down. Here's how to persist through this setback:

1. **Acknowledge the Setback**:
    - Accept that the business venture did not succeed and understand that failure is a part of the entrepreneurial journey.
2. **Analyze What Went Wrong**:
    - Conduct a detailed analysis of the venture's failure. Look at factors such as market demand, competition, product quality, marketing efforts, and financial management.
    - Identify specific issues, such as inadequate market research or ineffective marketing strategies, that contributed to the failure.
3. **Learn from the Experience**:
    - Extract valuable lessons from the analysis. For example, you might learn the importance of conducting comprehensive market research before launching a product or the need for a stronger online marketing presence.
    - Reflect on what you could have done differently and how these changes could have impacted the venture's success.
4. **Develop a Plan for Improvement**:
    - Create a detailed plan to address the identified issues. This could involve steps such as conducting thorough market research, developing a robust marketing strategy, and securing additional funding.

- Set specific, actionable goals for your next venture, such as validating the product-market fit before full-scale launch or building a more resilient financial model.
5. **Stay Positive and Motivated**:
    - Focus on the progress you've made and the knowledge you've gained. Keep a positive mindset by reminding yourself of your ultimate goals and the resilience you've developed.
    - Surround yourself with supportive peers, mentors, and resources that can help you stay motivated and inspired.
6. **Take Action and Move Forward**:
    - Apply the lessons learned to a new business venture or project. Use your improved skills and strategies to increase the likelihood of success.
    - Stay proactive and continue pursuing your entrepreneurial goals with renewed confidence and determination.

By persisting through setbacks and using them as learning opportunities, you can build resilience and continuously improve. This approach helps you stay motivated and focused on your long-term goals, turning challenges into valuable experiences that contribute to your overall success.

## The Importance of Adaptability and Learning from Failure

Adaptability and learning from failure are critical components of a risk-taking mindset. Being flexible and open to change allows you to navigate uncertainty and turn failures into valuable learning experiences.

**Steps to Enhance Adaptability**

## Stay Open-Minded

Being open-minded and willing to consider new ideas and approaches is essential for adapting quickly to new circumstances and seizing emerging opportunities. An open mindset allows you to be flexible, innovative, and responsive to change, which are crucial traits for success in a dynamic environment.

**Steps to Stay Open-Minded**

1. **Challenge Your Assumptions**: Regularly question your existing beliefs and assumptions. Be willing to reconsider and update them based on new information and perspectives.
    - **Example**: If you believe that traditional advertising is the only effective marketing strategy, challenge this assumption by exploring the potential of digital marketing and its impact on your target audience.
2. **Seek Diverse Perspectives**: Engage with people who have different viewpoints and experiences. Listening to diverse perspectives can broaden your understanding and inspire new ideas.
    - **Example**: Attend industry conferences, join networking groups, or participate in online forums where you can interact with professionals from various backgrounds.
3. **Experiment and Innovate**: Embrace experimentation as a way to discover what works

best. Be open to trying new methods, tools, and approaches, even if they are outside your comfort zone.
    - **Example**: If your marketing strategy isn't working, be open to experimenting with new tactics such as social media campaigns, influencer partnerships, or content marketing.
4. **Learn Continuously**: Commit to lifelong learning by staying updated with industry trends, advancements, and best practices. Continuous learning helps you stay relevant and adaptable.
    - **Example**: Take online courses, attend workshops, read industry publications, and follow thought leaders in your field to stay informed about the latest developments.
5. **Embrace Change**: View change as an opportunity rather than a threat. Being adaptable and flexible helps you navigate transitions smoothly and capitalize on new opportunities.
    - **Example**: If your company undergoes a reorganization, see it as a chance to take on new roles, learn new skills, and contribute to the organization's growth.
6. **Reflect on Experiences**: Regularly reflect on your experiences and the outcomes of your decisions. Use this reflection to learn and improve your approach.
    - **Example**: After implementing a new marketing tactic, reflect on its effectiveness and gather feedback to refine your strategy further.

**Example**

**Scenario**: Your current marketing strategy, which relies heavily on traditional advertising methods, is not yielding the desired results. Here's how to stay open-minded and adapt:

1. **Challenge Your Assumptions**:
   - Question the assumption that traditional advertising is the only effective method. Consider that digital marketing may offer better reach and engagement with your target audience.
2. **Seek Diverse Perspectives**:
   - Engage with marketing professionals who specialize in digital strategies. Attend marketing conferences, join online marketing groups, and seek advice from digital marketing experts.
3. **Experiment and Innovate**:
   - Be open to experimenting with new marketing tactics. Launch a social media campaign to see how it performs compared to traditional ads. Collaborate with influencers who align with your brand to tap into their follower base.
4. **Learn Continuously**:
   - Enroll in digital marketing courses to learn about the latest tools and techniques. Follow industry blogs and subscribe to marketing newsletters to stay informed about trends and innovations.
5. **Embrace Change**:
   - View the shift to digital marketing as an opportunity to modernize your approach and connect with a broader audience. Be flexible

and willing to pivot your strategy based on new insights.
6. **Reflect on Experiences**:
    - After running the social media campaign and influencer partnerships, analyze the results. Reflect on what worked well and what could be improved. Use this reflection to refine your marketing strategy.

By staying open-minded and willing to consider new ideas and approaches, you can adapt quickly to changing circumstances and seize emerging opportunities. This approach fosters innovation, flexibility, and continuous improvement, leading to greater success and resilience in a dynamic environment.

## Be Proactive

Anticipating potential changes and preparing for them in advance is key to staying ahead of challenges and adapting smoothly when they arise. Proactive planning allows you to mitigate risks, seize opportunities, and maintain a competitive edge.

### Steps to Be Proactive

1. **Stay Informed**: Keep up-to-date with industry trends, market developments, and regulatory changes. Regularly reading industry news, attending conferences, and networking with peers can help you anticipate potential shifts.
    - **Example**: Subscribe to industry publications, join professional associations, and follow thought leaders on social media

to stay informed about the latest developments.
2. **Conduct Risk Assessments**: Periodically assess potential risks and challenges that could impact your business or projects. Identify possible scenarios and evaluate their likelihood and impact.
    - **Example**: Conduct a risk assessment workshop with your team to brainstorm potential risks, such as supply chain disruptions, technological changes, or economic downturns.
3. **Develop Contingency Plans**: Create detailed contingency plans for the most likely and impactful risks. Outline specific actions to take in response to these scenarios and assign responsibilities.
    - **Example**: If you foresee industry changes due to new regulations, start developing compliance strategies before the regulations take effect. This might include updating your processes, training employees, and ensuring your systems are ready for compliance.
4. **Invest in Continuous Improvement**: Regularly review and improve your processes, systems, and skills. Being proactive about improvement helps you stay agile and responsive to change.
    - **Example**: Implement a continuous improvement program in your organization, where employees are encouraged to identify and suggest improvements to existing processes.
5. **Set Long-Term Goals**: Establish long-term goals and strategies that align with potential future scenarios. Long-term planning helps you stay

focused and prepared for changes in the business environment.
    - **Example**: Develop a strategic plan that includes goals for the next 3-5 years, considering potential industry changes and how your organization can adapt and thrive.
6. **Monitor and Review**: Continuously monitor the external environment and review your plans regularly. Adjust your strategies and contingency plans based on new information and evolving circumstances.
    - **Example**: Schedule quarterly strategy reviews to evaluate progress, reassess risks, and update plans as needed.

### Example

**Scenario**: You are a manager in a manufacturing company, and you foresee industry changes due to new environmental regulations that will take effect in the next two years.

1. **Stay Informed**:
    - Keep up-to-date with the latest news and updates on the upcoming environmental regulations. Attend industry conferences and participate in webinars focused on regulatory changes.
2. **Conduct Risk Assessments**:
    - Conduct a risk assessment to understand how the new regulations might impact your operations. Consider factors such as changes in production processes, additional compliance costs, and potential disruptions.
3. **Develop Contingency Plans**:

- Start developing compliance strategies well before the regulations take effect. This might include investing in new technologies that reduce emissions, training employees on new compliance requirements, and updating your environmental management systems.
- Create a detailed plan outlining the steps needed to achieve compliance, assign responsibilities, and set timelines for implementation.

4. **Invest in Continuous Improvement**:
   - Implement a continuous improvement program focused on sustainability and environmental performance. Encourage employees to suggest and implement process improvements that reduce environmental impact.
   - Regularly review your environmental performance and identify areas for improvement.

5. **Set Long-Term Goals**:
   - Establish long-term goals for environmental sustainability that align with the new regulations. Develop a strategic plan that includes goals for reducing emissions, improving energy efficiency, and achieving regulatory compliance.
   - Set measurable targets and milestones to track progress towards these goals.

6. **Monitor and Review**:
   - Continuously monitor the regulatory environment and stay updated on any changes or new developments. Schedule

quarterly strategy reviews to evaluate your progress towards compliance and update your plans as needed.
- Adjust your compliance strategies based on new information, feedback, and evolving industry standards.

By being proactive and anticipating potential changes, you can prepare your organization to adapt smoothly and stay ahead of challenges. This approach helps you mitigate risks, seize opportunities, and maintain a competitive edge in a dynamic business environment.

## Embrace Continuous Learning

Committing to lifelong learning by regularly updating your knowledge and skills is essential for staying relevant and adaptable in a rapidly changing world. Continuous learning allows you to keep pace with industry developments, innovate, and maintain a competitive edge.

### Steps to Embrace Continuous Learning

1. **Identify Learning Goals**: Determine the areas where you need to enhance your knowledge and skills. Set specific, measurable goals that align with your personal and professional development.
    - **Example**: Identify the need to improve your digital marketing skills to stay competitive in the marketing industry.
2. **Seek Diverse Learning Opportunities**: Explore various learning methods and platforms that suit your needs and preferences. These can include online courses, workshops, seminars, webinars, industry conferences, and books.

- **Example**: Enroll in an online course on digital marketing, attend a local workshop on social media strategies, and read the latest industry-related books.
3. **Create a Learning Schedule**: Allocate regular time for learning in your schedule. Consistency is key to making continuous learning a habit.
    - **Example**: Dedicate one hour each day to studying new digital marketing techniques or reading industry-related articles.
4. **Engage with Experts and Peers**: Network with industry experts and peers to gain insights and share knowledge. Join professional associations, participate in discussion groups, and attend networking events.
    - **Example**: Join a digital marketing professional association and participate in their online forums and local meetups to discuss trends and best practices.
5. **Apply What You Learn**: Implement new knowledge and skills in your work or projects. Practical application helps reinforce learning and demonstrates its value.
    - **Example**: Use the new digital marketing strategies you learned in your course to create and launch a social media campaign for your company.
6. **Reflect and Evaluate**: Regularly reflect on what you've learned and evaluate its impact on your performance. Identify areas for further improvement and set new learning goals.
    - **Example**: After launching your social media campaign, analyze its performance, gather

feedback, and identify areas where you can improve your skills further.

### Example

**Scenario**: You are a marketing professional looking to stay current with the latest trends and best practices in digital marketing.

1. **Identify Learning Goals**:
   - Set a goal to improve your digital marketing skills, specifically in social media marketing and content strategy.
2. **Seek Diverse Learning Opportunities**:
   - Enroll in online courses on platforms like Coursera, Udemy, or LinkedIn Learning that focus on digital marketing and social media strategies.
   - Attend local workshops or webinars hosted by industry experts.
   - Read books and articles by leading digital marketing professionals, such as "Jab, Jab, Jab, Right Hook" by Gary Vaynerchuk.
3. **Create a Learning Schedule**:
   - Set aside one hour each morning to complete an online course module or read an industry-related book.
   - Block out time in your calendar for attending monthly webinars or workshops.
4. **Engage with Experts and Peers**:
   - Join a digital marketing professional association, such as the American Marketing Association (AMA).

- Participate in online forums, LinkedIn groups, and local networking events to share knowledge and learn from others.
5. **Apply What You Learn**:
    - Implement the social media strategies you learned in your online course to create a comprehensive social media marketing plan for your company.
    - Use new content strategy techniques to enhance your company's blog and website.
6. **Reflect and Evaluate**:
    - After executing your social media marketing plan, review the analytics to measure its success.
    - Gather feedback from colleagues and supervisors on the impact of your new strategies.
    - Reflect on the experience, identify areas for further improvement, and set new learning goals, such as mastering advanced SEO techniques.

By embracing continuous learning, you can stay relevant, adaptable, and competitive in your field. Regularly updating your knowledge and skills ensures that you are prepared to navigate the challenges and opportunities of a rapidly changing world.

## View Failure as Feedback

Treating failures as valuable feedback that guides your future actions is crucial for continuous improvement and long-term success. Analyzing failures helps you understand what went wrong and how to improve, turning setbacks into opportunities for growth.

**Steps to View Failure as Feedback**

1. **Acknowledge the Failure**: Accept that the failure occurred and recognize it as a part of the learning process. Acknowledging failure helps you confront the situation and move forward constructively.
    - **Example**: If a product launch doesn't meet expectations, acknowledge that the launch didn't achieve its goals and prepare to analyze the reasons behind it.
2. **Conduct a Post-Mortem Analysis**: Gather your team to conduct a thorough post-mortem analysis. Review the entire process to identify what went wrong, what could have been done differently, and what was successful.
    - **Example**: Organize a meeting with your team to discuss the product launch. Use a structured format to review each phase of the launch, from initial planning to execution and outcomes.
3. **Collect Data and Feedback**: Gather data and feedback from various sources to get a comprehensive understanding of the failure. This can include metrics, customer feedback, team insights, and market analysis.
    - **Example**: Collect sales data, customer reviews, and feedback from your marketing and sales teams. Look at the market response and compare it to your expectations.
4. **Identify Root Causes**: Use the collected data and feedback to identify the root causes of the failure.

Determine whether the issues were related to planning, execution, market conditions, or other factors.
    - **Example**: Identify if the product's features didn't meet customer needs, if the marketing strategy was ineffective, or if external factors like economic conditions played a role.
5. **Develop Actionable Insights**: Translate the analysis into actionable insights. Identify specific changes and improvements that can be made to avoid similar failures in the future.
    - **Example**: Develop a list of actionable insights, such as refining the product features based on customer feedback, adjusting the marketing strategy to better target the intended audience, or improving team collaboration and communication.
6. **Implement Changes**: Put the identified improvements into action. Adjust your processes, strategies, and plans based on the lessons learned from the failure.
    - **Example**: Implement the changes in your next product development cycle. Update your marketing plan to incorporate the new strategies and ensure the team is aligned with the improvements.
7. **Monitor Progress and Adapt**: Continuously monitor the progress of the implemented changes. Be ready to adapt and make further adjustments as necessary based on ongoing feedback and results.
    - **Example**: Track the performance of the new product launch and gather feedback to ensure the changes are effective. Make

further adjustments if needed to achieve the desired outcomes.

### Example

**Scenario**: A product launch fails to meet expectations, resulting in lower-than-anticipated sales and customer dissatisfaction.

1. **Acknowledge the Failure**:
    - Accept that the product launch did not achieve its goals and prepare to analyze the reasons behind it.
2. **Conduct a Post-Mortem Analysis**:
    - Organize a meeting with your team to review the product launch. Use a structured format to evaluate each phase, from initial planning to execution and outcomes.
3. **Collect Data and Feedback**:
    - Gather sales data, customer reviews, and feedback from your marketing and sales teams. Look at the market response and compare it to your expectations.
4. **Identify Root Causes**:
    - Analyze the data to determine the root causes of the failure. Consider whether the product's features didn't meet customer needs, if the marketing strategy was ineffective, or if external factors like economic conditions played a role.
5. **Develop Actionable Insights**:
    - Translate the analysis into actionable insights. Identify specific changes and improvements to avoid similar failures in the future, such as refining the product features,

adjusting the marketing strategy, or improving team collaboration.
6. **Implement Changes**:
   - Put the identified improvements into action. Adjust your processes, strategies, and plans based on the lessons learned from the failure. For instance, refine the product development process to better align with customer needs and update the marketing plan.
7. **Monitor Progress and Adapt**:
   - Continuously monitor the progress of the implemented changes. Gather feedback to ensure the changes are effective and make further adjustments if needed to achieve the desired outcomes.

By viewing failure as feedback and using it to guide your future actions, you can turn setbacks into opportunities for growth and improvement. This approach helps you stay resilient, continuously learn, and ultimately achieve greater success.

## Practices to Cultivate a Risk-Taking Mentality

Cultivating a risk-taking mentality involves developing habits and practices that encourage boldness, creativity, and resilience.

### Practices to Foster a Risk-Taking Mentality

#### Set Bold Goals

Challenging yourself with ambitious goals that push you out of your comfort zone is essential for personal and professional growth. Bold goals inspire innovation and drive you to take calculated risks, fostering a mindset of continuous improvement and achievement.

**Steps to Set Bold Goals**

1. **Define Your Vision**: Start by identifying your long-term vision and what you ultimately want to achieve. This vision should be inspiring and align with your core values and passions.
    - **Example**: Your vision might be to become a leader in your industry, known for innovation and excellence.
2. **Break Down Your Vision into Specific Goals**: Translate your vision into specific, measurable, and time-bound goals. These goals should be ambitious yet realistic, providing a clear path to achieving your vision.
    - **Example**: Aim to expand your business internationally within the next five years.
3. **Assess Your Starting Point**: Evaluate your current situation, including your strengths, weaknesses, resources, and opportunities. Understanding where you are now helps you set realistic and achievable milestones.
    - **Example**: Assess your business's current market position, financial health, and readiness for international expansion.
4. **Create an Action Plan**: Develop a detailed action plan outlining the steps you need to take to achieve your bold goals. Include short-term and long-term actions, necessary resources, and potential challenges.
    - **Example**: Create a plan that includes market research, building international

partnerships, adapting your product or service for different markets, and securing funding for expansion.
5. **Set Milestones and Deadlines**: Break your bold goals into smaller, manageable milestones with specific deadlines. These milestones help you track progress and stay motivated.
    - **Example**: Set milestones such as completing market research within six months, establishing partnerships within a year, and launching in the first international market within two years.
6. **Stay Committed and Flexible**: Maintain a strong commitment to your goals, but be willing to adjust your plan as needed. Flexibility allows you to adapt to changes and overcome obstacles more effectively.
    - **Example**: Stay committed to international expansion, but be prepared to adjust your strategy based on market feedback and unforeseen challenges.
7. **Celebrate Progress and Successes**: Recognize and celebrate your achievements along the way. Celebrating progress reinforces the value of your efforts and keeps you motivated.
    - **Example**: Celebrate each successful milestone, such as securing your first international partnership or achieving your first sales in a new market.

**Example**

**Scenario**: You own a successful local business and want to set a bold goal to expand internationally within the next five years.

1. **Define Your Vision**:
   - Your vision is to become a globally recognized brand known for innovation and quality.
2. **Break Down Your Vision into Specific Goals**:
   - Aim to expand your business into at least three international markets within the next five years.
3. **Assess Your Starting Point**:
   - Evaluate your current market position, financial resources, and readiness for international expansion. Identify any gaps that need to be addressed.
4. **Create an Action Plan**:
   - Develop a detailed plan that includes conducting market research to identify target markets, building relationships with potential international partners, adapting your products for different cultural preferences, and securing funding for expansion.
5. **Set Milestones and Deadlines**:
   - Set milestones such as completing market research within the first six months, establishing international partnerships within the first year, and launching your product in the first international market within two years.
6. **Stay Committed and Flexible**:
   - Stay committed to your goal of international expansion, but be prepared to adjust your strategy based on market feedback, regulatory requirements, and other challenges that arise.

7. **Celebrate Progress and Successes**:
   - Celebrate each milestone, such as completing market research, securing your first international partnership, and achieving your first sales in a new market. Recognize the hard work and dedication that contributed to each success.

By setting bold goals and pushing yourself out of your comfort zone, you can inspire innovation, take calculated risks, and achieve significant growth. This approach helps you stay motivated, continuously improve, and ultimately reach your long-term vision.

## Take Small Risks Regularly

Building your risk tolerance by taking small, manageable risks regularly helps you become more comfortable with uncertainty and builds confidence. This practice allows you to experiment, learn from your experiences, and gradually increase your capacity to handle larger risks.

### Steps to Take Small Risks Regularly

1. **Identify Areas for Experimentation**: Determine areas in your work or personal life where you can experiment and take small risks. Focus on aspects where incremental changes can lead to improvements.
   - **Example**: Identify aspects of your product or marketing strategy that can be enhanced or tested on a smaller scale.
2. **Set Clear Objectives**: Define what you hope to achieve with each small risk. Setting clear

objectives helps you stay focused and measure the success of your experiments.
- **Example**: If experimenting with new product features, set objectives such as improving user engagement or gathering customer feedback.

3. **Start Small**: Begin with low-stakes experiments that do not require significant resources or have major consequences if they fail. This approach allows you to take risks without fear of significant loss.
    - **Example**: Test a new feature on a small subset of users or launch a limited-time marketing campaign on social media.
4. **Monitor and Analyze Results**: Track the outcomes of your experiments carefully. Analyze the data to understand what worked, what didn't, and why. Use this information to make informed decisions about future actions.
    - **Example**: Monitor user engagement and feedback on the new product feature or measure the effectiveness of the marketing campaign through metrics such as clicks, conversions, and sales.
5. **Learn and Iterate**: Use the insights gained from your experiments to refine and improve your approach. Continuous learning and iteration help you develop better strategies and build confidence in taking risks.
    - **Example**: If the new product feature receives positive feedback, consider expanding it to a larger user base. If the marketing campaign is successful, plan a

broader rollout with adjustments based on the initial results.
6. **Gradually Increase Risk Level**: As you become more comfortable with taking small risks, gradually increase the scale and complexity of your experiments. Building on your successes helps you develop a higher tolerance for risk.
    - **Example**: Move from testing product features on a small user group to conducting larger-scale beta tests, or expand your marketing experiments from social media to other channels like email or paid advertising.
7. **Celebrate Successes and Learn from Failures**: Recognize and celebrate the successes of your small risks. Equally, view failures as learning opportunities and analyze them to improve future experiments.
    - **Example**: Celebrate the positive impact of a successful new feature or marketing campaign with your team. If an experiment fails, conduct a debrief to identify lessons learned and apply them to future efforts.

**Example**

**Scenario**: You are a product manager looking to innovate and improve your product. To build your risk tolerance, you decide to take small, manageable risks regularly.

1. **Identify Areas for Experimentation**:
    - Focus on adding new features to the product and experimenting with different marketing strategies to boost user engagement.

2. **Set Clear Objectives**:
    - For the new product feature, the objective is to enhance user engagement and collect user feedback.
    - For the marketing strategy, the objective is to increase brand awareness and drive traffic to the website.
3. **Start Small**:
    - Introduce the new feature to a small group of beta testers to gather initial feedback.
    - Launch a short-term social media campaign targeting a specific audience segment.
4. **Monitor and Analyze Results**:
    - Track user engagement metrics such as feature usage, time spent on the feature, and user feedback.
    - Measure the effectiveness of the social media campaign by monitoring metrics like engagement rates, click-through rates, and conversions.
5. **Learn and Iterate**:
    - Based on user feedback, make improvements to the new feature and plan for a wider release if it proves successful.
    - Analyze the results of the social media campaign to understand what worked well and what can be improved for future campaigns.
6. **Gradually Increase Risk Level**:
    - Expand the beta testing to include a larger user base and consider rolling out the feature to all users if the feedback remains positive.

- Extend the marketing experiments to other channels, such as email marketing or paid advertising, based on the insights gained from the initial campaign.
7. **Celebrate Successes and Learn from Failures**:
    - Celebrate the successful implementation of the new feature with your team, acknowledging their hard work and contributions.
    - If the social media campaign did not meet expectations, conduct a post-mortem analysis to identify areas for improvement and apply those lessons to future marketing efforts.

By taking small risks regularly, you can build your confidence, become more comfortable with uncertainty, and develop a robust approach to innovation and improvement. This practice fosters a culture of continuous learning and adaptation, essential for long-term success.

## Surround Yourself with Risk-Takers

Spending time with people who embrace risk and innovation can greatly influence your mindset and behaviors. Their enthusiasm, resilience, and creative approaches can inspire and motivate you to take more risks and pursue bold ideas.

### Steps to Surround Yourself with Risk-Takers

1. **Identify Communities and Groups**: Look for communities, groups, or organizations where risk-takers and innovators gather. These can be

professional associations, networking groups, or online forums.
- **Example**: Search for local entrepreneur clubs, industry-specific meetups, or online platforms like LinkedIn groups or Reddit forums focused on entrepreneurship and innovation.

2. **Join a Mastermind Group**: Mastermind groups consist of like-minded individuals who support and challenge each other to achieve their goals. Joining such a group can provide you with valuable insights, feedback, and encouragement.
    - **Example**: Join a mastermind group of entrepreneurs who share their experiences, offer advice, and support each other's ventures. Look for groups that meet regularly, either in person or virtually.

3. **Attend Networking Events and Conferences**: Participate in events and conferences where you can meet and interact with risk-takers and innovators. These gatherings offer opportunities to learn from others and build valuable connections.
    - **Example**: Attend industry conferences, startup pitch events, or innovation summits to connect with like-minded individuals and hear from successful risk-takers.

4. **Engage in Online Communities**: Participate in online communities and forums where risk-takers discuss their experiences, challenges, and successes. These platforms can provide continuous inspiration and support.
    - **Example**: Join online communities such as Startup Grind, Indie Hackers, or specialized subreddits like r/Entrepreneur or r/Startups

to engage with risk-takers and learn from their journeys.
5. **Seek Mentors and Advisors**: Find mentors or advisors who are experienced risk-takers and innovators. Their guidance and advice can help you navigate your own risks and challenges more effectively.
    - **Example**: Reach out to successful entrepreneurs or industry leaders and ask if they would be willing to mentor you. Look for formal mentorship programs offered by professional associations or business incubators.
6. **Collaborate on Projects**: Work on projects or initiatives with risk-takers and innovators. Collaborative efforts can expose you to new ideas, approaches, and ways of thinking.
    - **Example**: Partner with a fellow entrepreneur on a new venture, join a collaborative research project, or participate in a hackathon or innovation challenge.
7. **Learn from Their Stories**: Read books, listen to podcasts, and watch interviews featuring successful risk-takers and innovators. Learning about their experiences can provide valuable insights and motivation.
    - **Example**: Read biographies of entrepreneurs like Elon Musk, Sara Blakely, or Richard Branson. Listen to podcasts like "How I Built This" or "The Tim Ferriss Show" to hear from risk-takers in various industries.

**Example**

**Scenario**: You are an aspiring entrepreneur looking to surround yourself with risk-takers and innovators to gain inspiration and support for your ventures.

1. **Identify Communities and Groups**:
    - Look for local entrepreneur clubs, industry-specific meetups, or online platforms focused on entrepreneurship and innovation. Join a local startup community or an online forum for entrepreneurs.
2. **Join a Mastermind Group**:
    - Join a mastermind group of entrepreneurs who meet regularly to share their experiences, offer advice, and support each other's ventures. Look for groups that match your industry or interests.
3. **Attend Networking Events and Conferences**:
    - Attend industry conferences, startup pitch events, and innovation summits to connect with like-minded individuals. Participate in events like Startup Weekend or industry-specific conferences.
4. **Engage in Online Communities**:
    - Join online communities such as Startup Grind, Indie Hackers, or specialized subreddits like r/Entrepreneur or r/Startups. Engage in discussions, ask questions, and share your experiences.
5. **Seek Mentors and Advisors**:
    - Find mentors or advisors who are experienced risk-takers. Reach out to successful entrepreneurs or industry leaders and ask if they would be willing to mentor you. Look for mentorship programs

through professional associations or business incubators.
6. **Collaborate on Projects**:
    - Work on projects or initiatives with risk-takers. Partner with a fellow entrepreneur on a new venture, join a collaborative research project, or participate in a hackathon or innovation challenge.
7. **Learn from Their Stories**:
    - Read books, listen to podcasts, and watch interviews featuring successful risk-takers. Read biographies of entrepreneurs like Elon Musk, Sara Blakely, or Richard Branson. Listen to podcasts like "How I Built This" or "The Tim Ferriss Show."

By surrounding yourself with risk-takers and innovators, you can gain valuable insights, inspiration, and support for your own ventures. This approach helps you develop a risk-taking mindset, encourages bold thinking, and fosters a culture of continuous learning and improvement.

## Reflect on Past Successes and Failures

Regularly reflecting on your past experiences to gain insights and build confidence is crucial for continuous improvement and informed decision-making. Understanding what worked and what didn't helps you make better decisions in the future and fosters a growth mindset.

### Steps to Reflect on Past Successes and Failures

1. **Keep a Journal**: Maintain a journal where you document your successes, failures, and the lessons

learned from each experience. Writing down your thoughts helps you process your experiences and provides a record to refer back to.
    - **Example**: After completing a project, write a journal entry summarizing the project's outcome, what went well, what challenges you faced, and the lessons learned.
2. **Set Regular Reflection Time**: Schedule regular times to reflect on your experiences, such as weekly or monthly. Consistent reflection helps you stay aware of your progress and areas for improvement.
    - **Example**: Set aside time every Friday afternoon to review your week, document your achievements and setbacks, and reflect on what you learned.
3. **Analyze Successes**: Reflect on your successful experiences to understand what contributed to the positive outcomes. Identify the strategies, actions, and behaviors that led to success, and consider how you can replicate them in the future.
    - **Example**: If a marketing campaign was successful, analyze the key elements that contributed to its success, such as targeting the right audience, using effective messaging, and choosing the appropriate channels.
4. **Examine Failures**: Reflect on your failures to identify what went wrong and why. Understanding the root causes of failures helps you avoid repeating the same mistakes and improves your problem-solving skills.
    - **Example**: If a project failed to meet its goals, examine the factors that led to the

failure, such as insufficient planning, lack of resources, or poor execution.
5. **Identify Patterns and Trends**: Look for patterns and trends in your successes and failures. Recognizing recurring themes can provide valuable insights into your strengths and areas for improvement.
    - **Example**: If you notice that most of your successful projects involved thorough planning and clear communication, make these practices a standard part of your workflow.
6. **Set Improvement Goals**: Use the insights gained from your reflections to set specific improvement goals. Focus on enhancing your strengths and addressing your weaknesses to continuously develop your skills and capabilities.
    - **Example**: If you identified a need for better time management, set a goal to implement time-tracking tools and techniques to improve your efficiency.
7. **Celebrate Successes and Learn from Failures**: Recognize and celebrate your achievements to build confidence and motivation. View failures as valuable learning opportunities and use them to grow and improve.
    - **Example**: Celebrate the completion of a successful project with your team, and conduct a post-mortem analysis for failed projects to identify lessons learned and areas for improvement.

**Example**

**Scenario**: You are a project manager who wants to improve your decision-making skills by reflecting on past successes and failures.

1. **Keep a Journal**:
    - Maintain a journal where you document each project's outcome, what went well, what challenges you faced, and the lessons learned.
2. **Set Regular Reflection Time**:
    - Set aside time every Friday afternoon to review your week. Document your achievements, setbacks, and reflections on what you learned.
3. **Analyze Successes**:
    - Reflect on successful projects to understand what contributed to their positive outcomes. Identify the strategies, actions, and behaviors that led to success.
    - Example: If a marketing campaign was successful, analyze the key elements that contributed to its success, such as targeting the right audience, using effective messaging, and choosing the appropriate channels.
4. **Examine Failures**:
    - Reflect on failed projects to identify what went wrong and why. Understanding the root causes of failures helps you avoid repeating the same mistakes.
    - Example: If a project failed to meet its goals, examine the factors that led to the failure, such as insufficient planning, lack of resources, or poor execution.

5. **Identify Patterns and Trends**:
    - Look for patterns and trends in your successes and failures. Recognizing recurring themes can provide valuable insights into your strengths and areas for improvement.
    - Example: If you notice that most of your successful projects involved thorough planning and clear communication, make these practices a standard part of your workflow.
6. **Set Improvement Goals**:
    - Use the insights gained from your reflections to set specific improvement goals. Focus on enhancing your strengths and addressing your weaknesses.
    - Example: If you identified a need for better time management, set a goal to implement time-tracking tools and techniques to improve your efficiency.
7. **Celebrate Successes and Learn from Failures**:
    - Recognize and celebrate your achievements to build confidence and motivation. View failures as valuable learning opportunities and use them to grow and improve.
    - Example: Celebrate the completion of a successful project with your team, and conduct a post-mortem analysis for failed projects to identify lessons learned and areas for improvement.

By regularly reflecting on your past successes and failures, you can gain valuable insights and build confidence. This practice helps you make better decisions in the future, fosters continuous improvement, and contributes to your overall growth and development.

## Inspirational Quotes and Affirmations

Inspirational quotes and affirmations can reinforce a risk-taking mentality by reminding you of the value of courage, perseverance, and resilience.

### Inspirational Quotes

- "Only those who will risk going too far can possibly find out how far one can go." – T.S. Eliot
- "The biggest risk is not taking any risk. In a world that's changing really quickly, the only strategy that is guaranteed to fail is not taking risks." – Mark Zuckerberg
- "Do not be too timid and squeamish about your actions. All life is an experiment. The more experiments you make, the better." – Ralph Waldo Emerson
- "Success is not final, failure is not fatal: It is the courage to continue that counts." – Winston Churchill

### Affirmations

- "I am capable of taking calculated risks and achieving great things."
- "I embrace challenges as opportunities for growth and learning."
- "I learn from my failures and use them as stepping stones to success."

- "I am resilient, adaptable, and confident in my ability to navigate uncertainty."

By developing a growth mindset, enhancing adaptability, practicing risk-taking behaviors, and reinforcing your mentality with inspirational quotes and affirmations, you can cultivate a strong risk-taking mindset. This mindset will empower you to face challenges head-on, embrace uncertainty, and achieve your goals despite the risks involved.

# Chapter 6

# Building a Support System

## The Role of Mentors, Peers, and Networks in Risk-Taking

A strong support system plays a crucial role in helping individuals take risks and achieve their goals. Mentors, peers, and networks provide guidance, encouragement, resources, and feedback, all of which are essential for navigating the uncertainties associated with risk-taking.

**The Benefits of Mentors**

- **Guidance and Advice**: Mentors share their knowledge and experience, helping you make informed decisions.
- **Accountability**: A mentor can hold you accountable for your goals and actions, ensuring you stay on track.
- **Networking**: Mentors can introduce you to valuable contacts and opportunities within their networks.
- **Confidence Building**: Having a mentor's support can boost your confidence, making it easier to take bold steps.

**The Benefits of Peers**

- **Shared Experiences**: Peers who are going through similar challenges can provide relatable insights and mutual support.

- **Collaboration**: Working with peers allows for collaboration on projects, sharing of resources, and collective problem-solving.
- **Motivation**: Peers can motivate and inspire each other to push beyond their comfort zones.

**The Benefits of Networks**

- **Access to Resources**: Networks offer access to information, tools, and resources that can aid in risk-taking endeavors.
- **Opportunities for Growth**: Networking events and groups provide opportunities for professional development and growth.
- **Supportive Community**: Being part of a network creates a sense of belonging and support, which is vital when facing risks.

## How to Find and Cultivate a Supportive Community

Building a supportive community involves identifying and connecting with individuals and groups that align with your goals and values. Here's how to find and cultivate a supportive community:

1. **Identify Your Needs**: Determine what type of support you need, whether it's mentorship, peer support, or access to resources and networks.
    - **Example**: If you're an entrepreneur, you might seek a mentor with experience in your industry, peers who are also building businesses, and networks that offer resources for startups.

2. **Join Professional Associations**: Become a member of professional associations related to your field. These organizations often provide networking opportunities, mentorship programs, and access to industry-specific resources.
   - **Example**: Join the local chamber of commerce, industry-specific associations, or entrepreneurship organizations.
3. **Attend Networking Events**: Participate in industry conferences, seminars, workshops, and networking events. These gatherings are excellent opportunities to meet potential mentors, peers, and network members.
   - **Example**: Attend events such as startup pitch nights, business expos, and industry conferences.
4. **Utilize Online Platforms**: Leverage online platforms and social media to connect with like-minded individuals and groups. LinkedIn, professional forums, and online communities can help you build a network even if in-person events are not an option.
   - **Example**: Join LinkedIn groups related to your field, participate in online forums, and follow industry influencers on social media.
5. **Seek Out Mentors**: Actively look for mentors who have the experience and knowledge you need. Approach potential mentors with a clear idea of what you hope to gain from the relationship and how you can contribute.
   - **Example**: Reach out to industry leaders, professors, or seasoned professionals and ask if they would be willing to mentor you.

6. **Build Relationships**: Cultivate relationships by being genuinely interested in others, offering support, and staying in regular contact. Strong relationships are built on mutual trust and respect.
   - **Example**: Follow up with new contacts after networking events, offer to help others with their projects, and stay in touch with periodic check-ins.

## Examples of Successful Support Systems

1. **Entrepreneurship Incubators**: Many successful startups began in incubators or accelerators where they received mentorship, resources, and a supportive community. Examples include Y Combinator and Techstars, which have nurtured numerous successful companies.
   - **Lesson**: Structured programs that provide comprehensive support can significantly enhance the success rate of new ventures.
2. **Professional Associations**: Organizations like the American Marketing Association (AMA) or the Project Management Institute (PMI) offer members access to a wealth of resources, including networking opportunities, certification programs, and industry insights.
   - **Lesson**: Being part of a professional association provides ongoing support and professional development.
3. **Peer Support Groups**: Mastermind groups and peer advisory boards bring together individuals with similar goals to share experiences, offer advice, and hold each other accountable. These groups

can be particularly effective for personal and professional growth.
    - **Lesson**: Regular interaction with peers who understand your challenges can provide crucial support and motivation.

## Tips for Giving and Receiving Support

**Giving Support**

1. **Be Available**: Offer your time and attention to those in your support network. Being available shows that you care and are willing to help.
    - **Example**: Schedule regular check-ins with your mentees or peers to discuss their progress and challenges.
2. **Listen Actively**: Pay close attention to what others are saying, ask clarifying questions, and show empathy. Active listening helps you understand their needs and provide relevant support.
    - **Example**: When a peer shares a challenge, listen without interrupting, and ask questions to fully understand their situation before offering advice.
3. **Offer Constructive Feedback**: Provide honest, constructive feedback that can help others improve. Focus on offering solutions and encouragement rather than criticism.
    - **Example**: If a peer's project has room for improvement, offer specific suggestions on how they can enhance their approach.

**Receiving Support**

1. **Be Open and Honest**: Share your challenges and goals openly with your support network. Being transparent helps others understand how they can assist you.
    - **Example**: When meeting with your mentor, openly discuss the difficulties you're facing and ask for specific advice or guidance.
2. **Act on Feedback**: Show that you value the support you receive by taking action on the advice and feedback given. Implementing suggestions demonstrates your commitment to growth.
    - **Example**: If your mentor suggests a new strategy, try it out and report back on the results.
3. **Express Gratitude**: Show appreciation for the support you receive. Acknowledging others' contributions reinforces the positive aspects of your relationships.
    - **Example**: Send a thank-you note or email to your mentor or peers, expressing how their support has helped you.

By building and nurturing a strong support system, you can enhance your ability to take risks and achieve your goals. Mentors, peers, and networks provide invaluable resources, guidance, and encouragement that make the journey of risk-taking more manageable and rewarding.

# Chapter 7
# Embracing Uncertainty

## The Benefits of Living with Uncertainty

Living with uncertainty can be daunting, but it also offers significant benefits. Embracing uncertainty fosters resilience, flexibility, and creativity, enabling you to navigate the complexities of life and work more effectively.

**Benefits of Living with Uncertainty**

1. **Enhanced Resilience**: Dealing with uncertainty builds mental toughness and resilience. It teaches you to adapt to changing circumstances and recover from setbacks more quickly.
    - **Example**: Facing the unpredictability of a new business venture can strengthen your ability to handle stress and bounce back from failures.
2. **Increased Flexibility**: Embracing uncertainty encourages flexibility and openness to change. This adaptability is crucial in rapidly evolving environments where rigid plans often fail.
    - **Example**: Being open to changing your marketing strategy based on real-time data can lead to more effective campaigns.
3. **Stimulated Creativity**: Uncertainty can spark creativity by pushing you to think outside the box and come up with innovative solutions to new challenges.

- **Example**: The need to pivot during a crisis can lead to the development of new products or services that better meet market demands.
4. **Opportunities for Growth**: Navigating uncertain situations often involves learning new skills and gaining experiences that contribute to personal and professional growth.
    - **Example**: Moving to a new country for work may initially feel uncertain, but it can lead to valuable cultural experiences and career advancements.

## Techniques for Staying Calm and Focused in Uncertain Times

Staying calm and focused during uncertain times is essential for making sound decisions and maintaining well-being. Here are some techniques to help you manage uncertainty effectively:

1. **Practice Mindfulness**: Mindfulness techniques, such as meditation and deep breathing exercises, can help you stay present and reduce anxiety about the future.
    - **Example**: Start your day with a 10-minute meditation session to center yourself and clear your mind.
2. **Focus on What You Can Control**: Concentrate on the aspects of a situation that you can influence and let go of what you cannot control. This approach helps reduce feelings of helplessness.
    - **Example**: If market conditions are unpredictable, focus on optimizing your

internal processes and improving customer service.
3. **Develop a Routine**: Establishing a daily routine provides a sense of stability and normalcy, even when external circumstances are uncertain.
    - **Example**: Maintain a consistent work schedule, exercise regularly, and set aside time for relaxation and hobbies.
4. **Set Small, Achievable Goals**: Break down larger tasks into smaller, manageable steps. Achieving these incremental goals can boost your confidence and keep you motivated.
    - **Example**: If you're launching a new product, set daily or weekly milestones, such as completing market research or finalizing the product design.
5. **Seek Support**: Reach out to friends, family, mentors, or support groups for guidance and reassurance. Sharing your concerns with others can alleviate stress and provide new perspectives.
    - **Example**: Join a professional network or peer support group where you can discuss challenges and exchange advice.

## Stories of Individuals Who Thrived in Uncertainty

1. **Steve Jobs**: When Steve Jobs was ousted from Apple, he faced significant uncertainty about his future. Instead of giving up, he founded NeXT and acquired Pixar, both of which became highly successful ventures. Eventually, he returned to Apple and led it to unprecedented success.

- **Lesson**: Embracing uncertainty and persevering through difficult times can lead to new opportunities and greater achievements.
2. **J.K. Rowling**: Before publishing the Harry Potter series, J.K. Rowling faced numerous rejections and financial struggles. She persevered through these uncertainties, and her books became a global phenomenon.
    - **Lesson**: Persistence and belief in your vision can help you overcome uncertainty and achieve extraordinary success.
3. **Elon Musk**: Elon Musk has faced countless uncertainties with ventures like SpaceX and Tesla. Despite numerous setbacks, he remained committed to his vision, resulting in groundbreaking achievements in space exploration and electric vehicles.
    - **Lesson**: Resilience and a long-term perspective can help you navigate uncertainty and drive innovation.

## Exercises to Practice Embracing Uncertainty

1. **Exposure Therapy**: Gradually expose yourself to situations that make you uncomfortable or uncertain. Start with small challenges and progressively tackle bigger ones.
    - **Exercise**: Try speaking up in meetings if you're usually quiet, or take on a project outside your comfort zone to build your tolerance for uncertainty.
2. **Mindfulness Meditation**: Practice mindfulness meditation to stay present and reduce anxiety

about the future. This exercise can help you remain calm and focused in uncertain situations.
    - **Exercise**: Spend 10 minutes each day practicing mindfulness meditation. Focus on your breath and let go of any thoughts about the past or future.
3. **Journaling**: Keep a journal to document your experiences with uncertainty. Reflect on how you felt, what you learned, and how you can apply these lessons in the future.
    - **Exercise**: Write about a recent uncertain situation you faced, how you dealt with it, and what you learned from the experience.
4. **Visualization**: Visualize positive outcomes to help reduce fear and build confidence in dealing with uncertainty. This technique can shift your mindset from anxiety to optimism.
    - **Exercise**: Spend a few minutes each day visualizing a successful outcome for a current challenge or project. Imagine the steps you'll take and the positive results you'll achieve.
5. **Gratitude Practice**: Focus on the positive aspects of your life by practicing gratitude. This exercise can help you maintain a positive outlook even in uncertain times.
    - **Exercise**: Write down three things you are grateful for each day. Reflect on why you appreciate these aspects and how they contribute to your well-being.

By embracing uncertainty and developing strategies to stay calm and focused, you can navigate the unknown with confidence and resilience. Learning from those who have thrived in uncertain times and practicing exercises to build your tolerance for uncertainty will help you grow and succeed in an ever-changing world.

# Chapter 8

# Measuring Success

## Redefining Success Beyond Traditional Metrics

Traditional metrics such as revenue, profit, and market share are important indicators of success, but they don't tell the whole story. To fully appreciate the impact of your efforts, it's essential to redefine success to include non-traditional metrics that reflect personal growth, learning, and overall well-being.

### Broader Definitions of Success

1. **Personal Growth and Learning**: Success can be measured by how much you've grown and learned from your experiences. This includes developing new skills, gaining knowledge, and increasing self-awareness.
    - **Example**: Successfully mastering a new software tool or language, even if it doesn't immediately impact your bottom line.
2. **Impact on Others**: Evaluate the positive impact you have on others, including employees, customers, and the community. Success can be seen in improved relationships, customer satisfaction, and contributions to social causes.
    - **Example**: Launching a community outreach program that benefits local schools or non-profits.

3. **Work-Life Balance**: Achieving a healthy work-life balance is a significant measure of success. It ensures long-term well-being and sustainability.
   - **Example**: Implementing flexible work schedules that allow you and your team to maintain a healthy balance between work and personal life.
4. **Innovation and Creativity**: Success can also be measured by the level of innovation and creativity you bring to your work. This includes developing new ideas, products, or processes that push boundaries.
   - **Example**: Introducing a novel product feature that significantly enhances user experience, even if it's still in the early stages of market adoption.
5. **Resilience and Adaptability**: Being able to adapt to changes and bounce back from setbacks is a crucial measure of success. It shows your ability to handle uncertainty and challenges effectively.
   - **Example**: Successfully pivoting your business strategy in response to market changes or unexpected obstacles.

## How to Evaluate the Outcomes of Risks

Evaluating the outcomes of risks involves more than just looking at immediate financial gains or losses. It requires a comprehensive analysis of the impact on various aspects of your personal and professional life.

**Steps to Evaluate Risk Outcomes**

1. **Set Clear Objectives**: Define what success looks like for each risk you take. This includes both quantitative and qualitative goals.
   - **Example**: For a new product launch, objectives might include achieving a certain number of sales, receiving positive customer feedback, and gaining market insights.
2. **Track Key Metrics**: Identify and track key metrics that align with your objectives. These can include financial metrics, customer satisfaction scores, and other relevant data.
   - **Example**: Track sales numbers, customer reviews, and market share growth for the new product.
3. **Assess Personal and Professional Growth**: Reflect on what you've learned and how you've grown from taking the risk. This includes new skills, knowledge, and experiences gained.
   - **Example**: Evaluate how the new product launch helped you learn about market trends, customer preferences, and product development processes.
4. **Evaluate Impact on Relationships**: Consider how the risk has affected your relationships with employees, customers, and other stakeholders.
   - **Example**: Assess whether the new product has strengthened customer loyalty or improved team collaboration.
5. **Analyze Long-Term Benefits**: Look beyond immediate outcomes to evaluate the long-term benefits of the risk. This includes potential future opportunities and strategic advantages gained.

- **Example**: Consider how the new product positions your company for future growth and innovation.

## Examples of Unexpected Successes

1. **Post-it Notes**: The invention of Post-it Notes by 3M was an unexpected success. Initially, the adhesive was considered a failure because it wasn't strong enough. However, it turned out to be perfect for creating removable notes, leading to a highly successful product.
    - **Lesson**: Sometimes, what seems like a failure can lead to an innovative and successful outcome if you remain open to new possibilities.
2. **YouTube**: Originally conceived as a dating site, YouTube's founders quickly realized its potential as a platform for sharing all kinds of videos. This pivot led to YouTube becoming the world's largest video-sharing platform.
    - **Lesson**: Being adaptable and open to changing your initial idea can result in significant unexpected success.
3. **Airbnb**: Airbnb started as a simple idea to rent out an air mattress in an apartment to make extra money. It evolved into a global platform that revolutionized the hospitality industry.
    - **Lesson**: Small, seemingly modest ideas can grow into transformative businesses through persistence and adaptation.

## Encouraging Readers to Celebrate Small Wins

Celebrating small wins is essential for maintaining motivation and recognizing progress. It helps build momentum and reinforces positive behavior.

## Steps to Celebrate Small Wins

1. **Set Incremental Goals**: Break down larger goals into smaller, achievable milestones. Celebrate each milestone as a significant step towards your ultimate goal.
    - **Example**: If your goal is to write a book, celebrate completing each chapter or reaching a word count milestone.
2. **Acknowledge Efforts and Achievements**: Take the time to recognize and appreciate your efforts and achievements, no matter how small. This helps maintain a positive mindset.
    - **Example**: After successfully completing a challenging project, take a moment to acknowledge your hard work and dedication.
3. **Share Your Successes**: Share your small wins with friends, family, or colleagues. Celebrating together can enhance the sense of achievement and provide additional encouragement.
    - **Example**: Share your progress on social media or during team meetings to involve others in your journey.
4. **Reward Yourself**: Treat yourself to a small reward to celebrate your achievements. This can be anything that makes you feel good and reinforces your hard work.
    - **Example**: After reaching a significant milestone, reward yourself with a nice dinner, a day off, or a favorite activity.

5. **Reflect on Progress**: Regularly reflect on your progress and the small wins you've achieved. This helps you stay focused on the positive aspects of your journey.
    - **Example**: Keep a journal where you document your small wins and reflect on how they contribute to your overall goals.

By redefining success, evaluating the outcomes of risks comprehensively, learning from unexpected successes, and celebrating small wins, you can create a more holistic and fulfilling approach to measuring success. This approach not only enhances your personal and professional growth but also helps you maintain motivation and resilience in the face of challenges

# Chapter 9

# Sustaining Momentum

## Strategies for Continuous Improvement and Risk-Taking

Sustaining momentum in your personal and professional life requires a commitment to continuous improvement and a willingness to keep taking risks. By consistently seeking ways to enhance your skills, processes, and strategies, you can maintain growth and stay competitive.

### Strategies for Continuous Improvement

1. **Adopt a Learning Mindset**: Continuously seek new knowledge and skills to stay ahead of trends and innovations. This mindset helps you adapt to changes and discover new opportunities.
    - **Example**: Regularly attend industry conferences, take online courses, and read relevant books and articles to keep your knowledge current.
2. **Implement Feedback Loops**: Create systems for regularly receiving and acting on feedback. This can help you identify areas for improvement and make necessary adjustments.
    - **Example**: Use customer feedback surveys and team debriefs after projects to gather insights and improve future performance.
3. **Set Incremental Goals**: Break down larger goals into smaller, manageable tasks that can be achieved incrementally. This approach helps

maintain momentum and provides a sense of accomplishment.
    - **Example**: If aiming to launch a new product, set goals for each phase, such as research, development, testing, and marketing.
4. **Foster a Culture of Innovation**: Encourage experimentation and creativity within your team. Create an environment where new ideas are welcomed and failure is seen as a learning opportunity.
    - **Example**: Implement innovation workshops and idea-sharing sessions to stimulate creativity and problem-solving.
5. **Regularly Review and Adjust Strategies**: Continuously monitor your progress and be prepared to adjust your strategies based on new information and changing circumstances.
    - **Example**: Conduct quarterly reviews of your business plan and adjust your strategies based on market trends and performance data.

## Avoiding Complacency and Staying Proactive

To sustain momentum, it's crucial to avoid complacency and remain proactive. Complacency can lead to stagnation, while a proactive approach ensures you are always moving forward and adapting to new challenges.

### Tips to Avoid Complacency

1. **Challenge the Status Quo**: Regularly question existing processes and strategies to identify areas for improvement. Don't settle for "good enough" when there's potential for excellence.

- **Example**: Conduct regular brainstorming sessions to explore new ways to improve efficiency and effectiveness.
2. **Set Stretch Goals**: Push yourself and your team with ambitious goals that require going beyond current capabilities. Stretch goals inspire innovation and higher performance.
    - **Example**: If your sales team consistently meets targets, set a higher target that challenges them to innovate and improve their approach.
3. **Stay Informed**: Keep up-to-date with industry trends, competitors' activities, and market changes. Staying informed helps you anticipate changes and adapt quickly.
    - **Example**: Subscribe to industry newsletters, follow thought leaders, and attend relevant webinars and conferences.
4. **Encourage Continuous Learning**: Promote a culture of continuous learning where team members are encouraged to develop new skills and knowledge.
    - **Example**: Provide opportunities for professional development, such as workshops, courses, and certification programs.
5. **Celebrate Milestones, Not Endpoints**: Recognize and celebrate progress, but emphasize that each milestone is a step toward ongoing improvement rather than a final endpoint.
    - **Example**: Celebrate reaching a project milestone, but remind the team that the next phase is just beginning and continued effort is needed.

## Long-Term Planning and Goal Setting

Long-term planning and goal setting are essential for sustaining momentum. By having a clear vision and roadmap for the future, you can stay focused and motivated.

**Steps for Effective Long-Term Planning**

1. **Define Your Vision**: Clearly articulate your long-term vision and the overall goals you want to achieve. This vision should inspire and guide your efforts.
    - **Example**: Develop a vision statement that encapsulates your ultimate goal, such as becoming a leader in sustainable technology solutions.
2. **Set SMART Goals**: Create Specific, Measurable, Achievable, Relevant, and Time-bound (SMART) goals that align with your vision. These goals provide a clear path forward.
    - **Example**: Set a SMART goal to reduce your company's carbon footprint by 50% within five years through specific initiatives.
3. **Develop a Strategic Plan**: Outline the strategies and actions needed to achieve your long-term goals. Include milestones, timelines, and key performance indicators (KPIs) to track progress.
    - **Example**: Develop a strategic plan that includes research and development, partnerships, marketing strategies, and financial projections.
4. **Regularly Review and Adjust**: Continuously review your progress and be prepared to adjust

your plan based on new information and changing circumstances.
    - **Example**: Conduct annual strategic reviews to assess progress, make adjustments, and set new priorities.
5. **Engage Your Team**: Involve your team in the planning process to ensure buy-in and collective commitment to the goals.
    - **Example**: Hold strategic planning workshops where team members can contribute ideas and understand their roles in achieving the vision.

## Inspirational Stories of Sustained Success

1. **Amazon**: From its beginnings as an online bookstore, Amazon has continuously evolved and expanded its business model. Through relentless innovation, customer focus, and long-term vision, Amazon has become a global e-commerce and technology giant.
    - **Lesson**: Continuous improvement, a willingness to take risks, and a long-term perspective can lead to sustained success and industry leadership.
2. **Nike**: Nike's commitment to innovation, branding, and customer engagement has driven its sustained success. By constantly pushing the boundaries of athletic performance and embracing new technologies, Nike remains a leader in the sports apparel industry.
    - **Lesson**: A strong brand identity, dedication to innovation, and deep understanding of

customer needs are key to maintaining momentum.
3. **Starbucks**: Starbucks has maintained its success through a combination of consistent quality, innovative offerings, and a focus on customer experience. By expanding globally and continuously evolving its product line, Starbucks has stayed relevant and popular.
    - **Lesson**: Consistency in quality, innovation, and customer-centric strategies can sustain growth and success over the long term.

By implementing strategies for continuous improvement, avoiding complacency, engaging in proactive planning, and learning from inspirational stories of sustained success, you can maintain momentum and achieve your long-term goals. This approach ensures ongoing growth, adaptability, and resilience in the face of challenges.

# Chapter 10

# Legacy and Impact

## The Long-Term Impact of Taking Risks

Taking risks often involves stepping into the unknown, but the long-term impact of these decisions can be profound and far-reaching. Risk-taking can lead to significant achievements, innovations, and positive changes that shape the future for individuals and society.

### Long-Term Impacts

1. **Innovation and Progress**: Many groundbreaking innovations and advancements result from taking risks. Without risk-takers, we would not have many of the technologies, medicines, and conveniences we enjoy today.
    - **Example**: The development of the internet, which has revolutionized communication and commerce, was a significant risk that paid off immensely.
2. **Personal Growth and Achievement**: Taking risks pushes individuals out of their comfort zones, leading to personal growth and the achievement of goals that might have seemed impossible.
    - **Example**: Pursuing an unconventional career path or starting a new business can lead to significant personal and professional fulfillment.
3. **Societal Change**: Risk-takers often drive societal change by challenging the status quo and advocating for new ideas and reforms.

        - **Example**: Social movements led by risk-takers, such as the Civil Rights Movement, have brought about significant progress in social justice and equality.
4. **Inspirational Influence**: The stories of those who take risks and succeed can inspire others to pursue their dreams and take their own risks.
        - **Example**: Entrepreneurs like Steve Jobs and Elon Musk inspire countless individuals to innovate and take bold steps in their own careers.

# How Risk-Taking Shapes Personal and Professional Legacy

Risk-taking can define your legacy, influencing how you are remembered both personally and professionally. The choices you make and the risks you take can leave a lasting impact on your industry, community, and the world.

### Shaping Your Legacy

1. **Defining Moments**: The risks you take often become the defining moments of your career and life. These moments can highlight your courage, vision, and determination.
        - **Example**: Launching a successful company or leading a groundbreaking project can become a central part of your legacy.
2. **Creating Value**: Taking risks that lead to the creation of value for others, whether through innovative products, services, or ideas, ensures that your impact is felt long after you are gone.

- **Example**: Inventors and innovators who create products that improve people's lives leave a lasting legacy of value and positive change.
3. **Inspiring Others**: By taking risks and achieving success, you set an example for others to follow. Your legacy can inspire future generations to pursue their dreams and take their own risks.
   - **Example**: Leaders who take bold steps to address global challenges can inspire others to contribute to these causes.
4. **Building Relationships**: The relationships you build and the people you influence through your risk-taking efforts can carry forward your legacy.
   - **Example**: Mentoring young professionals and helping them succeed can ensure that your values and knowledge are passed on.

## Stories of Influential Risk-Takers

1. **Nelson Mandela**: Mandela's risk of standing up against apartheid in South Africa, even at the cost of his freedom, led to profound changes in the country's political landscape and inspired a global movement for justice and equality.
   - **Lesson**: Taking a stand for what is right, despite personal risks, can lead to lasting positive change.
2. **Amelia Earhart**: As one of the first female aviators to fly solo across the Atlantic Ocean, Earhart took significant risks to challenge gender norms and advance the field of aviation.

- **Lesson**: Pioneering new paths can inspire others and break down barriers for future generations.
3. **Muhammad Yunus**: By founding the Grameen Bank and promoting microcredit, Yunus took a risk on an unproven financial model. His efforts have lifted millions out of poverty and earned him a Nobel Peace Prize.
    - **Lesson**: Innovative thinking and risk-taking in addressing social issues can lead to transformative impacts.

## Encouraging Readers to Think About Their Own Legacy

As you consider your own legacy, reflect on the impact you want to have and the risks you are willing to take to achieve it. Your legacy is shaped by the choices you make and the courage you show in pursuing your goals.

**Steps to Reflect on Your Legacy**

1. **Identify Your Values**: Determine what values are most important to you and how they align with your actions and decisions.
    - **Example**: If innovation and helping others are key values, focus on projects that drive progress and positively impact people's lives.
2. **Set Long-Term Goals**: Think about what you want to achieve in the long term and how these goals will contribute to your legacy.

- **Example**: Set a goal to mentor young professionals, launch a community initiative, or create a sustainable business model.
3. **Consider Your Impact**: Reflect on the potential impact of your actions on others and the world. Aim to create a positive and meaningful legacy.
    - **Example**: Evaluate how your business practices can contribute to environmental sustainability and social responsibility.
4. **Take Meaningful Risks**: Identify the risks that align with your values and goals and take them. Meaningful risks often lead to significant achievements and a lasting legacy.
    - **Example**: Take the leap to start a non-profit organization addressing a cause you are passionate about, despite the uncertainties.
5. **Document Your Journey**: Keep a record of your experiences, achievements, and the lessons you've learned. This documentation can serve as a testament to your efforts and inspire others.
    - **Example**: Write a memoir, start a blog, or create a video series sharing your journey and insights.
6. **Engage with Your Community**: Build and maintain relationships with those around you. Engage in activities that support and uplift your community, leaving a legacy of connection and support.
    - **Example**: Volunteer, participate in community events, and actively contribute to local initiatives.

By reflecting on the long-term impact of your actions, considering how risk-taking shapes your legacy, learning from influential risk-takers, and thinking about your own legacy, you can create a meaningful and lasting impact. Embrace the opportunities to take risks, pursue your passions, and leave a legacy that reflects your values and aspirations.

# Conclusion

## Recap of the Key Takeaways from the Book

Throughout "Crucial Risk Taking," we've explored the essential role that risk plays in personal and professional success. Here are the key takeaways:

1. **Understanding Risk**: Risk is an integral part of life and growth. It involves stepping into the unknown, which can lead to significant achievements and personal development.
2. **Overcoming Fear**: Identifying and addressing common fears related to risk, such as fear of failure, rejection, and the unknown, is crucial for taking bold steps.
3. **Calculated Risks**: Differentiating between reckless and calculated risks is essential. Using tools like SWOT analysis, cost-benefit analysis, and scenario planning can help assess and manage risks effectively.
4. **Building Resilience**: Embracing challenges, learning from criticism, celebrating effort, and persisting through setbacks are key strategies for building resilience and sustaining momentum.
5. **Support Systems**: The role of mentors, peers, and networks is invaluable in risk-taking. Cultivating a supportive community provides guidance, encouragement, and resources.
6. **Embracing Uncertainty**: Living with uncertainty fosters resilience, flexibility, and creativity. Techniques for staying calm and focused during uncertain times are essential for maintaining progress.

7. **Measuring Success**: Redefining success beyond traditional metrics, evaluating the outcomes of risks, and celebrating small wins help maintain motivation and recognize achievements.
8. **Sustaining Momentum**: Continuous improvement, avoiding complacency, long-term planning, and learning from inspirational stories of sustained success are crucial for ongoing growth.
9. **Legacy and Impact**: The long-term impact of taking risks shapes personal and professional legacy. Reflecting on your values and goals helps create a meaningful and lasting impact.

## Final Thoughts on the Importance of Risk-Taking

Risk-taking is not just about achieving extraordinary success; it's about embracing the journey of growth, learning, and transformation. Every risk taken is a step towards uncovering new possibilities, pushing boundaries, and discovering your true potential. The courage to take risks, face failures, and persist through challenges defines the path to meaningful accomplishments and a fulfilling life.

Risk-taking propels innovation, drives progress, and creates lasting change. It requires resilience, adaptability, and a willingness to learn from every experience. By embracing risk, you open yourself up to new opportunities and experiences that enrich your personal and professional life.

## Motivational Message to Empower Readers to Take Action

As you close this book, remember that the power to take risks and shape your future lies within you. The journey of risk-taking is not easy, but it is incredibly rewarding. Each step you take, no matter how small, brings you closer to your goals and dreams. Embrace the uncertainty, face your fears, and trust in your ability to navigate the challenges that come your way.

You have the strength, creativity, and resilience to overcome obstacles and achieve great things. Believe in yourself, stay committed to your vision, and keep moving forward. The path of risk-taking is filled with opportunities for growth, learning, and success.

## Call to Action for Readers to Start Their Own Journey of Risk-Taking

Now is the time to take action. Start your own journey of risk-taking and embrace the possibilities that lie ahead. Here are some steps to get you started:

1. **Identify Your Goals**: Reflect on your aspirations and set clear, bold goals that push you out of your comfort zone.
2. **Take Small Steps**: Begin by taking small, manageable risks that build your confidence and risk tolerance.
3. **Seek Support**: Surround yourself with mentors, peers, and networks that can provide guidance and encouragement.
4. **Stay Committed**: Persist through setbacks, learn from your experiences, and continuously seek improvement.

5. **Celebrate Progress**: Acknowledge and celebrate your achievements, no matter how small, to maintain motivation.

Remember, the journey of a thousand miles begins with a single step. Take that step today and embark on your path of risk-taking, growth, and success. Your future is shaped by the risks you take and the courage you show. Embrace the challenge, seize the opportunities, and create the legacy you desire.

---

Thank you for embarking on this journey with "Crucial Risk Taking." Your willingness to take risks and strive for greatness will lead you to a future filled with endless possibilities and remarkable achievements. Now, go out there and make your mark on the world.

## About the Author: P. A. Varro

P. A. Varro is a passionate advocate for personal growth and professional development. With years of experience in business, leadership, and innovation, Varro has dedicated his career to helping individuals and organizations unlock their potential through strategic risk-taking and continuous improvement. Drawing from a rich background in entrepreneurship and mentorship, Varro provides actionable insights and inspiring stories that empower readers to embrace uncertainty, overcome challenges, and achieve lasting success. Through his work, Varro aims to inspire a new generation of risk-takers to pursue their dreams and make a meaningful impact on the world.

www.ingramcontent.com/pod-product-compliance
Lightning Source LLC
Chambersburg PA
CBHW071917210526
45479CB00002B/449